T5-AFR-462

DUE DATE

TRADE SHOW EXHIBITING
The Insider's Guide for Entrepreneurs

TRADE SHOW EXHIBITING
The Insider's Guide for Entrepreneurs

Diane K. Weintraub

LIBERTY HALL
PRESS™

LIBERTY HALL PRESS books are published by LIBERTY HALL PRESS an imprint of McGraw-Hill, Inc. Its trademark, consisting of the words "LIBERTY HALL PRESS" and the portrayal of Benjamin Franklin, is registered in the United States Patent and Trademark Office.

FIRST EDITION
FIRST PRINTING

© 1991 by LIBERTY HALL PRESS, an imprint of McGraw-Hill, Inc.

Library of Congress Cataloging-in-Publication Data

Weintraub, Diane K.
Trade show exhibiting : the insider's guide for entrepreneurs / by Diane K. Weintraub.
p.   cm
Includes index.
ISBN 0-8306-0477-4   ISBN 0-8306-3585-8 (pbk.)
1. Exhibitions.   I. Title.
T396.W45   1991
659.1′52—dc20   91-2611
                                                    CIP

For information about other McGraw-Hill materials,
call 1-800-2-MCGRAW in the U.S. In other countries
call your nearest McGraw-Hill office.

Vice President and Editorial Director: David J. Conti
Technical Editor: Lori Flaherty
Production: Katherine G. Brown
Book Design: Jaclyn J. Boone
Cover photograph courtesy of Hall-Erickson.
LHP3

*To Gerry, all things are possible
because you are there.*

Contents

Acknowledgments

THERE ARE MANY PEOPLE WHO HELPED WITH THIS BOOK, DIRECTLY AND indirectly. I gratefully acknowledge the thousands of participants in the Exhibiting Skills Workshop who told their stories and shared their problems, many of which are included here.

Many, many thanks to Christine Christman for her help with the manuscript and to Gail Terry and Irene Kingston, who fearlessly typed and retyped all of the revisions.

A special nod of gratitude for the business guidance of Lee Knight, Publisher of *Exhibitor* magazine and producer of the Exhibitor Show; Dick Swandby, President of Exhibit Surveys; and Gordon Savoie, Chairman, Skyline Displays.

I have appreciated the valuable advice and information from Skip Cox, Vice President, Exhibit Surveys; Charlie McMillan, President, The McMillan Group; and Phyllis Fox and Ed Roberts, senior faculty members, Communique Exhibitor Education, Inc.

Thanks to all of you.

Preface

I THINK THAT TRADE SHOWS ARE THE MOST EXCITING AND VERSATILE WAY TO do marketing and selling available right now. They offer you an unparalleled opportunity for exposure to an entire market full of prospects and major decision makers. You get to see them face to face, tell your story, and see their reaction in the short timespan of a few minutes—and that's exciting.

At shows, you can lay your message at the feet of all the industry opinion makers at once. Members of the press go to shows to cover those making the news. Industry bigwigs go to shows intent on doing deals. Financial analysts go to shows shopping for high profile, hot companies to put on their "buy" list. Images have been made at trade shows, and images have been broken at trade shows.

Shows are exciting moments in the lives of industries. Some are even milestones. I remember seeing Steven Jobs, then-president of Apple Computer, talking with Mitch Kapor, Mr. Lotus Development Corporation, at a software show the year before Lotus released Jazz. The move that Lotus would later make with Jazz was foretold at that show for all to see. It's thrilling to see business history being made right before your eyes.

But many exhibitors, especially small or new exhibitors, often don't feel that excitement or they don't believe that they can benefit from it. They are wrong. They, too, can be part of it, can tap into it. They are just the ones who should be making history, creating an image, and doing deals. It is especially for them that this book is written.

Introduction

MOST EXHIBITORS SPEND MORE TIME PICKING OUT A PAIR OF SHOES THAN they do picking the shows where they spend thousands of dollars. So it's not surprising that 40 percent of all first-time exhibitors are so disgusted by the experience that they never exhibit again. Yet others profit, some fantastically. Why? What's the difference between the two?

Let me tell you how one company increased its profits dramatically by going to trade shows. Jane sculpted and was very good at it. Her interest was lifelike sculptures of people, especially small children, so she combined her dressmaking abilities with her sculpting to produce absolutely exquisite dolls.

Her husband, Ed, was very impressed and excited when he discovered that people would pay a few hundred dollars each for the dolls. He had an entrepreneurial spirit so he tried a few swap meets and doll hobby shows and found that there was a sizable interest. Soon, Ed quite his job and devoted himself full-time to growing the doll business. It took off, and at the end of the first year, he was spread so thin that there was no time to make the sales calls the business needed to expand.

About that time, Ed received an exhibitor's prospectus for a giftware show. Ed thought about the economics of letting gift store owners come to him instead of paying to see them, so he signed up. It cost them about $3,000 to exhibit and they booked $175,000 in business in the three days of the show.

Four years later (and remember the company is only five years old), Ed and Jane's business attends 18 shows annually and books an average of $250,000 in business per show. That's $4.5 million, plus the orders that come in after the shows, which adds up to the $6 million in annual sales revenue. And they still only invest $3,000 per show.

How can this happen for you? If you are a busy marketing or sales manager, advertising/promotions manager, or a small business owner or manager, this book will show you ways to immediately increase your revenue through trade shows, as Ed and Jane did. First, it will show you the most direct way to immediately increase sales from trade shows so that you aren't wasting time on efforts that don't work. Second, it will point out the pitfalls and ripoffs discovered by others, thereby saving you money.

You'll learn how to make smart decisions about selecting the right shows, pinpointing the right space, and setting clear objectives. You will find out about exhibit design and how exhibits communicate. You will be guided through the show services package and learn about the intricacies of setup on the show floor and cost containment.

You will explore the finer points of powerful communications throughout the trade show selling process. You will see lead forms, lead tracking, and measurement techniques. You will hear about how to use promotions to bring traffic to your exhibit and how to use in-booth, traffic-building activities. And you will get a clear picture of how to work with, and use, the press at shows.

You won't feel overwhelmed by too much detail or theory. I know that if this book is going to work for you, it has to contain easy-to-read, useful information—information that you can put right to work to increase sales and market share.

That's how the book is organized, too. If you want to, and you have the time, you can read it through from cover to cover. If not, skim the chapters that are most important to you and look for the tables and checklists. These contain the really critical information that will help you make smart decisions and keep you out of trouble.

After reading this book and applying the information in it, you'll be able to pick a show or booth space from a floor plan and feel confident that you aren't missing any good shows or getting stuck with bad space. You'll feel in control when negotiating space contracts, too.

You will know exactly how much each show contributed to your bottom line and precisely what the return on investment was for each show. You'll know where your dollars are going and what they are doing for you.

You will understand how to buy an exhibit, getting good value for the investment. You will be sure that it does the three critical jobs every exhibit must.

You will feel comfortable and in control during setup on the show floor because you understand the forms in the exhibitors kit and know who the players are and where to go for help. You will know how to keep the lid on expenses and feel confident when you trim the fat, leaving only the lean portion of your budget.

After reading the chapters on promotion, you'll be able to bring lots of traffic made up of decision makers right to your booth. After reading the chapter on selling skills, you'll feel comfortable and in control talking with visitors. You will be able to speak to visitors with confidence and help them to feel at ease with you as you work with them to pinpoint the ways your products and services fit into their need.

Ever pass an exhibit jammed with people and wonder why they were able to attract a crowd and you weren't? Some people look so confident at setup. They know what needs to be done and where to go for it. Ever wonder what they know? Do you have a competitor you want to outshine on the show floor? This book is designed to give you all the insider's tips, including how to bring a crowd to your booth and be effective with them once they're there.

Trade shows can contribute substantially to your bottom line, and this book will show you the way.

Part I
The mechanics

1

Selecting the right shows

QUICK, ANSWER THIS QUESTION: WHY DOES YOUR COMPANY EXHIBIT AT trade shows?

A very memorable participant in our seminar on trade show management said that one show on his schedule was chosen because the marketing manager liked to ski. An unbelievably bad reason to select a show!

Plenty of exhibitors go to shows because they are afraid of not being there. In this chapter, we'll look at some of the most common, *wrong* reasons to exhibit at a show—the myths. You will find out what to do about getting out of a show that's not profitable for you and how to deal with pressures to be in those shows. Then we'll turn to the right way to pick a show. We'll cover how to analyze show data and judge it for its honesty. Finally, you'll learn exactly how to evaluate the shows you are considering to determine if they are worth the investment.

Two common myths

Let's take a look at the mythical—not scientifically based—reasons for exhibiting at shows. These are the very worst reasons for putting a show on your schedule, and you need to be aware (and wary) of them. But be warned, like the tale of the Lost Dutchman Mine, many of them are fake, but have a ring of truth to them.

Myth #1: They'll talk about us if we're not there

One of the most common myths is the fear that, if an exhibitor drops out of a show, they will be missed, and that people, especially the competition, will talk negatively about them. "They'll say that we are going out of business or are having rough financial times."

Reality: Most people won't miss you and, if they do, they probably won't assume the worst. Even if a few do, you definitely won't go out of business.

Look at what the big companies do. Most of them participate in, or drop out of, shows as they see fit and the competition be hanged. Each year, General Electric, for example, selects its shows very carefully based on their own merit and never worries about the negative impact of dropping out. Apple Computer has always participated in or dropped out of shows as it pleased. In the early days, every time they dropped out, the competition would say that Apple was going through rough times. Perhaps, as they say about any publicity being good publicity, the overall effect was to keep Apple in the limelight.

Reality: To be a leader, you must act like a leader. IBM, AT&T, and GE have always had the confidence to drop out of a show if the results were disappointing. They all operate from a position of strength and act confidently when deciding to drop out. Sure, they're very big, but size isn't the main factor. Leadership and acting with confidence is. If you decide not to participate or to drop out of a show, be sure to communicate your reasons to your employees so they can be ready with a statement should anyone ask why the company was not there. Never exhibit at a show just because the competition does. There are better ways to decide if a show is worth participating in.

The larger your company and the more you use advertising, the less likely it is that your image will suffer if you don't exhibit. This is especially true if you enjoy the many benefits of having a leadership position in a particular market. One research report showed that 18 percent of a show's audience reported they had been in the IBM exhibit, and IBM wasn't even at the show! This can be attributed to the ever-present power of the IBM image and its ability to appear to be everywhere at once, including a show it never attended. (In case you are wondering, the research was triple-checked and found to be rock solid and absolutely sound.)

Myth #2: We must support the association

Some exhibitors feel that it is mandatory for them to exhibit at the industry association event. This can be a complex issue, and in order to sort it out properly, you must first identify exactly who is exerting pressure on you and then determine if it is legitimate. First, where is this pressure to exhibit coming from? Is it coming from the association? From your clients? From within your company? From within your industry?

Reality: They might be conning you. Perhaps they don't even represent a legitimate association. An example of a high-pressure tactic that is rare and completely out of line is the bogus fire- or police-support organization that is just a boiler-room scam. When my company was in New Jersey, we were pestered by a caller who intimated that it would be in our best interest to buy space in a directory and sponsor a booth at a fair in support of the local police department. Fortunately, we checked the show out, and the local police knew nothing about it. These pressure tactics are extremely rare, but still, be on guard for them.

Reality: The association is conning you. Often, someone will tell you that if you don't attend the show, when it comes time for member firms to pass out the contracts, your company will be left out. If you are a small or relatively new company, this threat of industry disfavor can be rattling.

Be a realist. Most associations do not control the purchasing decisions of their member companies. Although an association might promise that their membership will give you some preferential treatment when your salesperson calls, they are promising something that they cannot deliver—buyer loyalty.

Reality: Someone within your company is conning you (and themselves, too)? The pressure to exhibit can also come from within your own organization. Sometimes, an overzealous or desperate sales manager will take the position that, "We just need to be there to be seen." Can you help him or her jell-up that statement? Is the reason for exhibiting to get leads or to improve image? Being seen sounds like an image objective, although it might mean being seen by the right people; those who will leave their names for follow-up, and that's a lead-gathering objective.

In this case, the best plan of action is to help whomever is pressuring you to identify precisely how the event will help your company achieve either image objectives or sales goals.

Locating and evaluating shows

Now that you have seen the wrong reasons for putting a show on your schedule, let's take a look at the right reasons. In this section, you'll find out how to locate shows and determine if they are right for you, as well as how to compare shows.

Locating shows

Many exhibitors have an uncertain feeling that they might not be attending the right shows and are missing other trade show opportunities. If this describes you, you need to know a simple method for finding the right shows. Although it is always wise to periodically check for new shows and evaluate your schedule whenever new products are released, additional market niches are identified, or extensions for product life cycles are sought, there

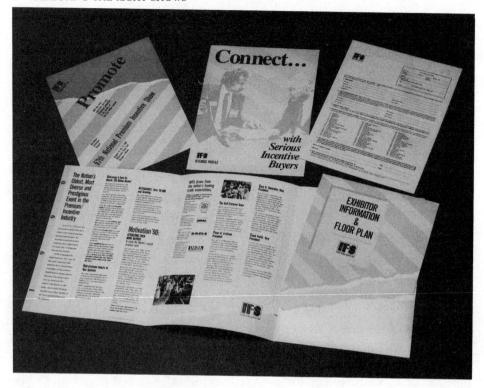

Fig. 1-1. A typical show prospectus.

is a simple, three-part process for locating and evaluating show opportunities:

1. *Check trade show directories.* Three of the largest show directories are:

   Trade Show Week Data Book
   245 West 17th Street
   New York, NY 10011
   (800) 521-8110

   Trade Show and Professional Exhibits Directory
   Gale Research
   Book Tower
   Department 77748
   Detroit, MI 48277
   (313) 961-2242

Health Care Exhibitors Association Directory
5775 Peachtree Dunwoody Rd.
Atlanta, GA 30342
(404) 252-3663

Just check the trade publications serving the markets you are targeting, then contact the show's management and request a prospectus, which contains the statistics you'll need to analyze the show. Figure 1-1 shows a typical show prospectus.

2. *Check local sources.* Often, major directories don't list local shows. In this case, try these sources:
~Chapters of national organizations
~Associations
~Chambers of commerce
~Visitors and convention bureaus
~Facilities, such as civic centers and hotels.

3. *Compare and contrast show statistics.*

Evaluating shows

The most important aspect of show evaluation is carefully reviewing the type of audience the show owners are likely to deliver to you, the exhibitor. As you review the prospectus, Fig. 1-1, it is important to keep your focus on the audience analysis and ignore the glitz. There are two ways to proceed when evaluating shows and the audiences they deliver:

1. *Who is the audience?* Compare the prospect profile to the attendee profile using the title or job description. Are these people worth spending the money to talk to?

2. *What does the audience buy?* Identify the number of attendees who are interested in buying your products and services, and answer the question, "Are these people worth seeing because many have an interest in our products and services?"

Evaluating the audience

One of the major strategies in the "Getting into the right show" game is to match the profile of your target audience as closely as possible to the audience's profile. The closer the match, the better the show can help you to achieve your objectives.

The place to start is, of course, by identifying your target audience. Which decision makers do you wish to reach when you are participating in shows to achieve sales goals? Which opinion makers do you wish to reach when you are striving for image objectives?

As you will find out in chapter 7 on planning, trade shows, like other marketing communications media, can only do two things. It can help you sell products and services or it can help build your image. You must choose which is the primary task. No effort can serve two masters successfully, and for trade shows, as for all marketing communications efforts, the choice is between leads/sales or image.

Once you have chosen between leads/sales or image, you will need to draw up a profile, by title or job description, of the groups you are targeting. For example, at printing products shows it is quite common to see multiple levels of buyers. At these shows, you will find 1.) owners of printing plants, also called economic buyers because they often make buying decisions based on the economic impact to the company; 2.) shop supervisors, called technical buyers because they are concerned with the technical impact of the purchase on their domain; and 3.) pressmen, or user buyers, who are concerned about how easy the equipment is to actually use. All three groups will come into the exhibit, as seen in Fig. 1-2, and all three seek different information, any one of which might be the final decision maker. Try your skill at simple show selection based on the decision-maker profile shown in Example 1-1.

If you could only exhibit at one show, you would need to decide if it was more important to reach the 5,000 owners or the 7,000 supervisors and pressmen. However, you might decide to invest in both events to completely cover your market.

Note that, if you did go to both shows, you would probably want to change the exhibit's emphasis from the economic concerns of your targets at the Print-It Show to the technical and user orientation of your targets at Ink Inc. Expo.

Determining what attendees buy

As in the printing products shows shown in Example 1-1, reaching your target audience is the name of the game and matching target profiles is an excellent approach. However, there is an even more direct way to go: by determining the number of attendees that are interested in your products and services. In this section, we will work through a 30-minute exercise designed to answer the question, "Is this show good for me?"

Four steps to show analysis.

Buying plans and product interests are critical in determining a show's value just as circulation is in advertising. After all, you would not want to advertise in a publication that went to people who had no interest in your product or service. Similarly, you need to avoid shows that have a high percentage of

Fig. 1-2. At this printing products show, exhibitors found economic buyers, technical buyers, and user buyers.

_____ **Example 1-1.** _____
Show Profile Exercise

Which of these two fictitious shows would you select if you want to reach the largest number of buyers? Why?

Print-It Show		Ink Inc. Expo	
Owners, CEOs	5,000	Supervisors	4,000
Purchasing agents	3,500	Consultants	1,000
Sales/Marketing	3,000	Pressmen	3,000
Students	500	Sales/Marketing	2,000
Total	12,000		10,000

Notice that Ink Inc. Expo delivers 2,000 fewer attendees than the Print-It Show. However, if you look at your target audience—owners, shop supervisors, and pressmen—the numbers are as follows:

Print-It Show		Ink Inc. Expo	
Owners, CEOs	5,000	Supervisors	4,000
		Pressmen	3,000
Total	5,000		7,000

non-buyers and seek out shows that have high numbers of buyers for your products and services.

Some show sponsors have researched their attendees to determine their buying plans and product interest, but most don't. Even those that do must be questioned on the source of their data. Here are four steps to evaluating the quality of the data offered by show management.

Step 1: Is the source of the data reputable?   What is the source of the data? You will be making some expensive decisions based on what the show promoter tells you, and you need to feel confident that the information is reliable. I've heard of a situation where a show owner found that he had a shrinking show on his hands and took some desperate measures.

Over the period of a few years, it seemed that he spent all of his time trying to make the attendance numbers look good rather than discerning the cause of the diminished attendance. The first thing he did was to fire the highly reputable firm that was auditing the event, supposedly as an economy measure, and put in its place a company that makes badges, a registration firm. The show then based its attendance figures on the number of names registered for the show.

Sounds all right, except for the fact that the show's owners purchased a mailing list of 20,000 names and ran them through the registration system. Therefore, the number of people registered for the show was quite a bit higher than the actual number of people in attendance. When reviewing show statistics, remember that it is very important to know the precise source of the data you are being offered.

Step 2: What should you do if there is no data?   Many shows do not survey their attendance to determine product interest, so the best you will get is a prospect profile of title and geographic distribution. Still, others offer neither the prospect profile nor the product interest analysis. In these cases, you are buying a "product" that cannot be described, and you, the buyer must beware.

New shows, of course, will have no data to offer because the statistics are always based on the previous year's performance. In these cases, it is advisable to ask the show promoter how he intends to promote the event and how much he plans to spend doing it. Some exhibitors have a policy that they will not participate in a new show because show dollars are too precious to risk on an unproven event. Other firms, wanting to be the leaders, jump in the first time.

Shows that make no attempt to analyze their audiences of past years are of three types: those that are unsophisticated, fat cats that don't care, and crooks. The unsophisticated usually run small shows of local or regional interest and probably, if they think of surveying a show at all, think it is only for the big shows. Fat cats sport a take-it-or-leave-it attitude and often run very successful events, making no excuses for their lack of data. The crooks,

like the unethical found in all lines of business, don't want you to know what
you are buying.

It's unfortunate for you, the exhibitor, because all three might have a
show that's right for you, but you'll never know, or a least you'll never know
based on data. The fact-finding mission becomes much more complex without hard data. If you cannot get data then you must rely on sleuthing.

There are some ways to find out about a show when you can't get reliable data from the show manager:

1. *Call other exhibitors.* Call at least eight to ten exhibitors, and ask how
   the show was for them. Be sure to poll a good cross section so your
   information is not skewed by product interest or size of exhibit. Also,
   ask them to guess at profile percents, like what percent were owners
   and what percent were technical, etc., as well as product interest.

2. *Call your competitors.* Depending upon your relationship with the
   competition, this could be risky or informational.

3. *Call your exhibit suppliers.* Ask them if they could put you in contact
   with other clients who go to the show or if they could find out how
   the show went. Companies that do exhibit set-up are often a wealth
   of information and can give you their opinions on how the show was
   run. They are often the first to hear the unvarnished comments of the
   floor manager about attendance. Remember, if you use any of their
   statements when talking to show management, be sure to protect
   your sources.

4. *Call promotion managers.* Ask for the publications that serve your
   targeted industry to see if they have exhibited at the show, and if so,
   what were their findings.

5. *Go yourself.* If you want to get the very best information on the
   show—attend yourself. Walk the show, talk to exhibitors and attendees alike.

Step 3. Discarding non-buyers.   The first thing to do in evaluating
the viability of any show is to take the gross attendance and eliminate the
non-buyers such as exhibitors, students, consultants, and spouses. Non-
buyers are individuals who, by their very category, will never purchase from
you. Before eliminating any group, however, be certain that they *are* non-
buyers and not influencers that you do want to reach. For example, many
construction companies are owned by husband and wife teams and the
spouse often plays a key buying role. (See Fig. 1-3.) There are other hidden
influences as well.

For example, an exhibitor who sells herbicide attended an agricultural
show, and in the pre-show meeting, overheard many of the sales reps com-

plaining that the 4H'ers and Future Farmers of America wasted their time by asking a lot of questions. These sales representatives needed to ask themselves how long it would be before they will be calling on these same people as farm owners. These kids usually come from farm families where agriculture is the family business. Rather than being looked at as a nuisance, these students were just another opportunity.

Another group that you will want to think carefully about is the exhibitors. Can you sell to them as well? (The best time to do this is the last, very slow, day of the show or to set up an appointment beforehand.) In eliminating the non-buyers, don't be too quick to discard any group without thinking it through.

Step 4. Estimating the prospects.   You have arrived at the very heart of this chapter: judging the value of a show based on the best estimate of the number of prospects for your products or services.

If show management has provided you with good data on the number of prospects you can expect, then the task is easy. However, as mentioned

Fig. 1-3. Be careful when categorizing spouses as nonbuyers. At this construction show, it was fairly common to see husband and wife company owners involved in the decision making.

before, most shows do not. In the event that you have no data about the show, you will still be able to estimate the number of prospects for your products and services by using a statistical average.

According to Exhibit Surveys, Inc., the leading research firm in the United States, Canada, and the United Kingdom, and based on more than 25 years of data, 16 percent of the attendees at an average show will be interested in any given product or service. Let's go over that again. For any single product or service displayed on the show floor, an average of 16 percent of the show audience will be interested in that product or service.

People usually react with a raised eyebrow to this statement, because it is such a generality. Remember that 16 percent is just the average of many types of products and services at many shows and, as such, it is simply a starting point. It can and should be adjusted. How much should you adjust the 16 percent? Start by taking a very close look at the shows that do offer research and compare the product interest statistics from those events. Do you spot trends among certain show types? Shows that attract a vertical audience, all operating room nurses, for example, are likely to have higher product interest percents for many of the products exhibited. Research from shows that attract diverse audiences, like the premiums shows, will indicate lower product interest percents. If you know this, and remember that 16 percent is just the average, then you can begin to fine-tune the numbers.

Fine-tuning the product interest percent

When you are using the 16 percent average product interest percent, there are three tips for adjusting it:

1. *By Geography.* Can you discern what percent of the total attendance is outside of your area of distribution? If many of the prospects are unreachable because of distribution, you'll probably want to reduce the 16 percent.

2. *By Show Scope.* Is the scope of the show, the subject matter of interest, narrow or wide? For example, is it a sporting goods show (wide scope) or an aerobics show (narrow scope)? For a show with a wide scope, but you are offering a narrow range product, you will want to reduce the 16 percent.

3. *By Experience.* If you find that similar shows where research is available quote a much higher or lower interest percent for your products or services, use that data as your guide. Check to be certain that the events are similar and attract the same type of audience, however.

How important is past experience?

Each exhibitor's past experience is highly overrated as a basis for show participation success. Few exhibitors make a well-planned and executed effort so it is difficult to determine if their results are an accurate reflection of the show and not simply a reflection of their efforts. Is it the show that was bad or their exhibit or promotions?

Many show owners and managers have shared their frustrations and commented about the scores of exhibitors who arrive late, try to set up the exhibit in the opening hours of the show, sit and read or chat with each other for three days, and then say the show was "no good." I used to joke about a fictitious person reading *War and Peace* at an exhibit, until I did see a woman at a show at McCormick Place in Chicago actually reading that book. Now the joke is more sad than funny.

If you can honestly say that your show effort was a good one, only then can you count on the accuracy of the results as being good input for the evaluation process.

Can I expect many visitors?

No matter how well you researched a show, the actual number of visitors you've targeted to visit your exhibit will probably not be realized. It is just not human nature for all of the people you've targeted to make it to your exhibit even though they are interested in your products or services. Some might choose to play golf or stick with the seminar sessions; still others have an interest but don't have the energy to walk all of the show floor; or they might simply look the other way when they do walk by and miss you.

The percent of the audience that is likely to make it to your exhibit varies from show to show, as does the product interest percent. There is, however, an actual measurement of how motivated a particular show audience is to see what is on the floor—the Audience Interest Factor (AIF). The AIF is a widely used industry measurement of the percent of the show audience that stops to talk or pick up literature at two out of 10 exhibits.

The AIF varies from show to show and ranges from a low of about 30 percent to a high of about 60 percent. If you desire to get an even closer estimate of the actual number of people who might visit your booth, reduce the final calculation shown in Fig. 1-4 by 50 percent.

To go or not?

Only you can make the final decision about participating in a show, and only you can decide if it will be worth your company's investment. The following says it all:

---

1. What is the source of the data?
   Do I trust that it is truthful?
   ( ) Yes ( ) No (Deduct 10% from attendance)

2. How many nonbuyers are there?
   Gross attendance   _____
   Less nonbuyers   − _____
   Equals net attendance _____

3. Is product interest data available?
   ( ) Yes   ( ) No
   (Use actual product interest %)   (Use 16%)
   Net Attendance _____   Net Attendance _____
   × Prod. Interest: × _____%   × Prod. Interest: × _____%
   Prospects _____   Prospects _____

4. Can I fine-tune? (see Fine-tuning the Product Interest)
   By geography?   + or − ? _____
   By show scope? + or − ? _____
   By exposure?   + or − ? _____
                            Adjustment _____

5. Will that many visitors actually come to my exhibit?
   Is research available on the interest level of the attendees?
   ( ) Yes. Use actual audience   ( ) No. Reduce by 50%
        interest factor
   Prospects   Prospects
   (adjusted) _____   (adjusted) _____
   AFI   × _____%   AFI   × _____50%
   Potential traffic _____   Potential traffic _____

Fig. 1-4. Follow these five steps for calculating your potential audience at each of the shows you are considering.

1. What are the number of prospects you will reach?   _____
2. What will you have to invest to reach them?   _____
3. Is 1. worth 2.?   _____

If you want a quick calculation for arriving at your rough investment in step 2, try five times the cost of space if you are using a custom exhibit and three times the cost of space if you are using a portable exhibit.

Your investment in show participation is considerable. Here is a triple check to help you feel confident that your decision is a sane one.

1. *Can You Reach This Audience Any Other Way?* If your objectives are predominantly image objectives, does advertising or public relations make sense instead? If your goal is leads, can it be more economically reached with direct mail?

2. *Do You Really Need An Exhibit?* If you only need to reach 10 key decision makers, you could get a suite and invite them to a private

presentation. Think of this: for the cost of a custom exhibit, you could hire a yacht! Be careful though, some shows black-list you if you try to get a suite at the official hotels but don't take an exhibit.

3. *Are There Better Shows?* Shop around and keep in mind the printing products show examples. All shows are not equal.

For the most part, making the decision about a show is boring, lonely, dull work—that *must be done.* You don't have to put up with that nagging feeling that there are better shows out there and you're missing them. Don't stop looking around until you feel confident that you found all of the right shows and made the right decisions. Only then will you feel solid about the shows you are attending and positive that they are well worth the investment you make in them.

2

Selecting the best space

MOST EXHIBITORS FIND THAT THEY ARE NOT SELECTING EXHIBIT SPACE BUT that it is being assigned to them. Do you feel that you have too little choice in the matter and don't always know what's going on? Do you have a craving for highly visible space up front but always end up back in the corner by the rest room? If this describes you, then you need the information in this chapter. Once you understand the typical space assignment practices used by most show managers and know what to do about them, you'll start to get the space you want.

In this chapter, you will discover how to determine the amount of exhibit space you need. If you buy too much, you'll be wasting money. If you buy too little, there won't be enough room for all of the prospects for your products and services, which means you'll be missing valuable leads. You'll learn an easy-to-use, six-step strategy for picking space at the shows where you do have a choice of locations.

Space assignment practices

The way each show decides on who gets which bit of real estate is something you must know. All shows differ slightly, but there are some commonly used practices. There is an important distinction between an *assignment*, which is made for you by the show manager and *selection*, whereby you pick the space you desire. The following are some of the most common methods space is chosen. They are ranked in order from most common to least common.

Priority point system.   This method for space assignment is the fairest. It is based on a point system where points are awarded for the total square feet of space taken over the years. Frequently, one point per ten feet of space taken in each year of participation will give larger, more established companies taking large spaces the advantage over smaller, newer firms. This method is often used by larger shows.

If this is how a particular show you are interested in is arranged, the best you can do is to check your point tally (and that of your competitors) to be certain you are getting your fair share.

The lottery.   The lottery system facilitates the priority point system. Exhibitors are called together at a meeting and asked to make their selection, in a given order, based on points accrued. Although it sounds orderly, the selection event is often quite competitive and you need to develop a strategy for getting the space you want.

Here's how it works. Each exhibitor is assigned a specific time to come pick space. If the exhibitor misses the assigned time slot, they are usually put all the way at the bottom of the list, or at least at the bottom of the list for their time block. Usually, you will be given a specific amount of time in which you must make your selection, otherwise they move on and you lose your turn. Therefore, you must be prepared to make your selection quickly when called.

Before going to the selection meeting, take a floor plan and "X" any spaces that would be acceptable to you. If you are at the top of the list to choose at your appointed time, you might prioritize your selections so that you can quickly make other choices. It is a good idea to "X" quite a few, you might find that many have been taken. Be sure to show up a little early so you can get organized. Mark off the spaces that have been taken and note where the competition is located, then go ahead and make your selection.

First date/postmark.   This is one of the oldest assignment practices. Priority is given to the earliest postmark, or the first application with a deposit check to reach the office. The facsimile machine makes this race to be first all the more interesting. Some shows now accept faxed space contracts while others do not, so you will want to find out how the show handles faxes.

Follow the rules carefully and call show management to be sure you understand all of the factors they are going to consider in making their assignments. Will they be looking at postmarks or will they be time stamping the applications as received? This practice, as well as others, give show management more control over the placement of exhibitors on the floor, and it is not uncommon to find them playing favorites.

Grandfather assignments.   These assignments stay the same from year to year, never changing unless an exhibitor drops out. Obviously, this system can only be used when the show is in the same place each year.

Stay in touch with show management to let them know you are very interested in upgrading your space. Ask what they typically do if an exhibitor drops out, and discuss how your need might fit into their system. Grandfather assignments are often used by shows that have more exhibitors than the hall will accommodate, but for whatever reasons, the show has not moved to another site. Often, the show is sponsored by an association in which change happens slowly, if at all, or the owner of the show has a very "sweet" deal with the facility.

Show management decides.   In this situation, the criteria for making site assignments are foggy at best and simply boil down to the fact that show management does as it likes. Sometimes, they make every possible effort to be fair, other times they play favorites or, rarely, even look for payoffs to give preference in making the assignments.

Communicate often with show management, on the phone and in person. If you are going to be in the vicinity of their offices, by all means, stop by to visit or to take the people to lunch. Listen for clues on how space assignments are made, and be especially aware of hints that it will take a little private money on the side to get what you want. (Once the hint is dropped by them, you can decide what you want to do about it, but either way, at least you know where you stand and how decisions are really made.)

When considering space assignment practices, you come out ahead if you know exactly how the show assigns its space and then take every clever measure possible to work that system for all it is worth. Table 2-1 summarizes space assignment/selection practices.

A final hint about space deposits and contracts: read the contracts carefully and pay the deposit on time. Late payments can run you the risk of losing that space or your priority points.

Table 2-1.
Space Assignment/Selection Practices Summary

System	Priority point	Lottery	First Date/ Postmark	Grand father	Show management
Type	Selection	Selection	Selection/ assignment	Assignment	Assignment
Comments	Fair	Fair, but competitive			
	Check the point tally.	Be organized. Be early or on time.	Understand the rules. Check Faxes and hand-delivered.	Communicate your needs.	Understand the criteria. Communicate your needs.

Avoiding bad space

What is bad space? How do you determine if the space you are assigned is unacceptable, and what should you do if it is? "Bad" space is any location that puts you at a competitive disadvantage. Space that is too small, such as the broom closet the sponsors are calling "the annex," the rotunda, or otherwise off the mainstream of traffic is a candidate for the bad space title.

This is not to say that any other location except the main hall is a poor choice. In fact, some shows tend to ramble from meeting room to meeting room or building to building and the attendees embrace the layout with the same enthusiasm attendees at a county fair would, seeking out all the nooks and crannies. Most shows are not that lucky when they spin off their floor plan into the foyer, parking garage, or tents. As you look at the floor plan, ask yourself, "If you were an attendee, what would motivate you to go to the adjacent areas?" If shuttle buses, signs, luncheon breaks, or seminar sessions won't move them in your direction, it is probably bad space.

Bad space can be acceptable if it is the only space you can get and you must be at the show. In this situation, understand that the responsibility to bring the traffic to your area is all yours, and you will not be helped by the natural flow of traffic.

What to do about bad space

The best thing you can do if you have bad space is to be vocal, but not a complainer, and give the show manager a good reason to upgrade your space. They probably won't do it just because you don't like your location, but they will listen hard to requests for changes that are substantiated by sound business logic. Here are two classic examples.

A small group within a large company wanted to get into a show that had been sold out for years. They were stuck on a waiting list for any available space and were eventually assigned a 10 x 10 foot-booth, which they gladly took even though they needed a 50 x 70-foot exhibit space. Shortly after the assignment was made, the marketing manager visited the show manager. Over lunch, she shared with the show manager the highlights of their confidential plan to enter this market. A key part of the plan was this show. The show manager was flattered that this prestigious company had been so open with him and promised to do what he could. When a large company that also exhibits at the show was acquired by another company and their space became available, it was assigned to the exhibitor. When a show manager can see your needs as you see them, that's the first step to getting what you want.

Here's another example. A small computer components company took a 10 x 20-foot space at an industry show. Each year, they were assigned space in the back and at the side of the hall but traffic just didn't make it to them in great numbers. The advertising manager took the occasion of a new product release to petition for space in a more central location. He explained to the show manager that the new product would have broader appeal and needed broader exposure, hence a more advantageous location on the show floor. They too got just what they asked for.

The conclusions here are obvious. If you have a logical, strategic business reason for requesting a change in the space you have been assigned, then talk to show management. But chances are they won't go out of their way just because you don't like the space they gave you.

Determining how much space you need

No matter how the space is assigned, you have to tell show management how much you want. Have you thought about how much space you are going to need? Why you need that amount? For some exhibitors, the minimum increment of 10 feet, or one booth, is about all they can afford, and perhaps all they need. If you have not been through the space calculation process before, however, then now is the time to do it. Only after you have calculated the space you'll need will you feel confident that you are not buying too much space and wasting money or not buying enough and missing visitors because they can't fit into a crowded booth.

For the small exhibitor who feels lucky just to have made the investment to be in the show, the thought of buying more space might seem out of the question. If you are in this situation and find that your exhibit is often very crowded, you are probably missing people because your exhibit is too small to handle the target audience for your products at this show. If this describes you, be sure to follow this section carefully, because when you do stop to calculate the prospects you are missing, you might reconsider.

Space calculation is a simple process. In a nutshell, you figure out how many people might come into your exhibit and how much space it will take to accommodate all of them. Calculations for this are based on the number of hours and size of the show, but mostly, on how many people are interested in your products. (If you have been through chapter 1, *Selecting the right shows*, this should be easy.)

Let's take a look at that again. You should be contracting for a booth that is large enough to accommodate all of the prospects for your product that are walking the show floor. Remember, if it's too small, they won't fit, and if it's too large, you are wasting money.

Be advised that the methods presented here are streamlined. The absolutely correct way to do it is just a bit longer and requires more analysis of the show audience, especially use of the audience interest factor. (If you want to do it properly, just follow the notation under number three.)

While the long way of doing it is the preferred way, you can sometimes spend the better portion of the rest of your life trying to get accurate statistical information from some show managers and promoters. What you really need is a short version that cuts some corners—and saves a lot of time—but will still give you usable figures to work with. The short version is as follows:

1. Calculate the net attendance. Net attendance is the total number of attendees less those who, by their category, are obviously non-buyers. This would include exhibitors, consultants, spouses, or students. Check show statistics for gross attendance and discard non-buyers to give you the net attendance.

2. Calculate what percent of the audience you think will have an interest in your product. The average is 16 percent (see chapter 1). If yours is a mature product, there might be less interest. Likewise, if it is a new product, there might be greater interest. If the product has appeal to only a small number of the attendees at this particular event, then the percent will drop. (Also, see chapter 1, *Fine-tuning the product interest percent*, for information on adjusting the product interest percent.

3. Multiply net attendance by product interest and then divide that number in half. What you are doing is first figuring out the number of prospects for your product at the show by multiplying the net attendance by the product interest percent. That gives you an estimate of prospects at the show. It is unrealistic, however, to expect that all of them will make it to your exhibit. By dividing the number of prospects in half, you are being more realistic. If you want to do the long version of this, see chapter 1, *Can I expect many visitors?*

4. Use Table 2-2 to determine the amount of space you will need. The table is designed so that if you know the number of prospects and hours of the show, you can quickly see how much space and how many staffers you'll need. Under each listing, the first number indicates square footage of exhibit space and the second number indicates the number of staffers needed.

Table 2-2 also works backwards, and if you really do not have the time or patience to deal with space calculation, there is a short cut:

1. Find the column for the right number of hours at the show you are going to.

2. Follow it down to the size space you think you need. If there is more than one entry, as there is for 100 square feet, go to the last entry.

3. The far left column will show you how many prospects you will be able to handle throughout the show in that size exhibit. Does that

_____ **Table 2-2.** _____
Space Calculation

Show hours	5	10	15	20	25	30	35	40
Number of visitors								
500	300+/6+1	150/3	100/2	100/2	100/2	100/2	100/2	100/2
1000	600/23	300/6	200/4	150/3	100/2	100/2	100/2	100/2
2000	1300/26	600/13	400/8	300/6	200/5	200/4	200/4	150/3
3000	2000/40	1000/20	600/13	500/10	400/8	300/6	200/5	200/5
4000	2500/53	1300/26	800/17	600/13	500/10	400/8	400/7	300/6
5000	3300/66	1600/33	1100/22	800/16	600/13	500/11	400/9	416/8
6000	4000/80	2000/40	1300/26	1000/20	800/16	600/13	500/11	500/10

+   *square footage needed.*
+ +   *staffers needed.*

sound right based on either your own experience or the information you have from show management? Keep two important things in mind as you consider this number. First, only those interested in your products or services will come to the exhibit and second, of the total number interested in what you are showing, only about half of them ever make it to your booth.

If you are thinking in terms of leads and not traffic, these numbers might seem too high. This is because this number includes those visitors who might simply have walked by, or into, the exhibit, regardless of whether they spoke with your staffers and requested follow-up.

Seven steps to selecting your exhibit space

On every exhibit space contract there is a place to indicate which space you want. If you are in a position to select and get the booth space you want, consider yourself lucky. If you think that there is a relatively strong chance that you might actually get that space, then before you even fill out the contract, familiarize yourself with the rest of this chapter, which will guide you through a seven-step process for picking space.

If you are sure you don't have a chance of getting the space you really want, you can just write a note on the contract requesting them to call you when it comes your turn to pick. When they call, ask what spaces of the size and type that you need are left. Then follow the seven steps for picking space presented here.

Step 1: Where are the entrance and registration areas?

Before determining where the entrances and registration areas are, first take a good long look at the floor plan and familiarize yourself with it. Some are big, some are small, but all of them will give you plenty of information if you take the time to look. (Fig. 2-1 shows several floor plans.)

The strategy behind being near the entrance is that it is where the registration area usually is and the attendees will see you every time they come and go. They will also see you right away, which is when they are at their freshest, are not yet overloaded with information, and before their feet hurt so badly they don't want to talk to you for more than two seconds.

This strategy can be useful when it is very important to make an immediate impression on visitors, such as at events where attendees are likely to go for only one of the show days. For example, research on the conference for automotive engineers held annually in Detroit indicates that a high percentage of attendees come for just one day. Therefore, if you do not make a good impression on that particular day, you lose your only opportunity. If you exhibit at a show like this, then you must strategize exactly where on the floor the visitors are likely to be at their freshest, but more on this later.

A very real advantage in being close to the entrance is that attendees will pass your exhibit each time they enter or leave the hall. This will give you

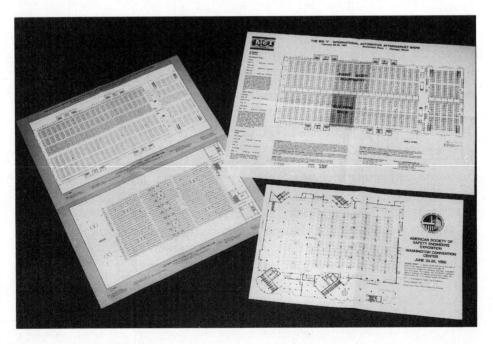

Fig. 2-1. Sample floor plans.

greater exposure, not only will it provide increased opportunities to talk to attendees, but it provides increased opportunities for them to see your exhibit and be impressed by it or get interested in its message.

This is, however, based on the assumption that the floor plan of the hall is laid out so that attendees enter and leave through one main exit. If seminar sessions, luncheons, receptions, and the like can be reached through another egress that will change the traffic pattern, you must take that into consideration as well.

There's another issue involved in being up front: can you be up front? The layout of the hall and size of the booth space you require might prevent you from being front and center. Quite often, the show floor is laid out so that the large spaces are near the entrance, which makes the show look impressive. Although most show managers try to pepper them throughout the hall, the small spaces end up around the sides and back. If you want a 10 x 10-foot booth, you probably won't see one in the front row.

Another factor is the priority system used by the show manager. You might find that the show you want to attend has a strict system in place and that your ranking is too low on the list to get the space you really want. In this case, there is no chance of being up front.

Traditionally, only the largest and longest-running exhibitors have exhibited in the front of the hall, so there is a certain cache in being up front. Surprisingly, there are special times when that can be a legitimate objective:

- You want visitors to see you each time they enter and exit, assuming that there is only one way to come in and leave.
- You feel it is important to make an immediate impression on visitors. An example is a show where attendees go for just one day.
- You can be up front because you have an advantage in the space assignment process.
- The layout of the hall makes it possible for you to be up front.

Step 2: How will traffic flow from the seminars?

Certain booth locations can be better because they are close to traffice flow coming from the seminar sessions. Attendees have their thinking stimulated after a seminar session, and if you can talk to them right away, they are highly receptive to what you have to say. For that reason, take a close look at the seminar sessions schedule and locations to better anticipate the coming and going of the attendees.

Here's an example of how we have used the seminar programs at shows at which we exhibit regularly. One show is very social, and we tend to see many of the same people year after year. We find that key decision-makers seldom make it to the exhibit hall or spend very little time there. The seminar sessions do not drive this conference but the social events do, so we do not consider the ebb and flow of traffic from the seminar sessions at this event when selecting exhibit space.

By contrast, we exhibit at another conference where traffic to the seminar sessions is an important factor in the selection of our exhibit space. Here the seminars drive the event, are very well attended, and are the talk of the conference. When the seminars let out, the attendees are ready to take actions and make decisions on the issues that have been discussed in the sessions. In other words, they are all fired up. At this show, we try to get space near the entrance closest to the seminar meeting rooms.

Some shows have meal functions, like a luncheon buffet, or social functions, like a cocktail reception, in areas of the exhibit hall. These events can impact traffic flow positively and should also be considered when choosing space.

Consequently, review the show schedule carefully to determine how the seminar program is arranged, if it is strong, and meal or social functions are likely to impact traffic flow. Both can be important factors in picking your exhibit space.

Step 3: Where are the visitor lounges?

Being close to the visitor lounges set up by show management is advantageous because visitors can gaze at your exhibit while they relax. There is a second advantage in that your staffers can also use the lounge as a conference area, which is a big asset if you have a small exhibit.

Open lounges where attendees can sit and chat, rest, or in cases where show management is generous, have a complementary coffee and donut, tend to draw heavier traffic than adjacent aisles. With a lounge close to your exhibit, the attendees have time to sit, think, and relax. They are at rest with their defenses down, and when they look your way are more open to your message.

In addition to the increased traffic and exposure, the biggest benefit to a location next to the lounge is your ability to use it as a conference area. If your exhibit is short on space, that lounge could be a big help. Remember, when you do use the lounge, don't be away from your booth for too long. A lounge also makes a nice place for your exhibit staffers to take a break. It is within view and you can get them back fast. (See Fig. 2-2.)

Step 4: How does traffic flow to and from the facilities?

Sooner or later, everyone uses the snack bars and rest rooms. You need to locate these on the floor plan and decide how, or if, they impact traffic flow.

*Fig. 2-2. Being near a lounge can be such an advantage that this exhibitor spon-
sored one and included a product message panel in it.*

First consider the rest rooms. Are they all in one location? If they are, you
could get added exposure as visitors find their way to them. If there are rest
rooms in many locations, as there are on most show floors, not everyone will
be using one path to get to them, so rest room location isn't an important
factor in making your space selection decision.

Being close to the food service areas can be advantageous because attendees will pass your exhibit on the way to eat and might even stare at it
while they stand in line. You will need to consider whether the food service
indicated on the floor plan is just a snack bar where people will spend very
little time on an infrequent basis, or whether it is a dining area that doubles
as a lounge. If it is the latter, then be sure to consider it in the same way as a
lounge, mentioned in Step 3.

If you do choose a location next to the snack bar, be prepared to be a
good neighbor of casual dining. Here's an example where an exhibitor was
not. At a construction industry show, an exhibitor featuring cement trucks
was right next to the snack bar, which had no place to sit down. They were
very pleased to have this particular space so close to the snack bar because
they felt that traffic had to go right past them.

Because many construction firms are family-owned businesses, this
show was attended by decision makers and their families. As it grew closer to
lunch time, first a few and then many of the families took their chili dogs and

greasy burgers and sat down to picnic on the exhibitor's big expanse of white carpet immediately adjacent to the snack bar. The exhibitor was horrified and quickly rented stanchions to block the end of the booth. Before they could put the stanchions in place, however, the exhibitor had to chase away the crowd of happy family picnickers, now growing to very large proportions. The sternest, most serious of the staffers bullied all of the families out of the booth and instantly created a very negative image among this highly qualified audience.

In conclusion, when reviewing the floor plan, consider rest rooms only if they are all in one area of the hall and consider food service areas if you can use them as a lounge and are willing to put up with any inconvenience they might cause.

Step 5: Where is the competition?

Nothing lights a fire under us like the competition. Of course, you must be aware of competitors and the locations of their booth space. But should you be near them or away from them? If a comparison between your products and theirs is to your advantage, then request a location close to them. If comparison is not in your best interest, then stay away. At this point, it might be helpful to refer to the material on tactics in chapter 7 on planning, especially the examples that elaborate on attacks for making a move on the competition and defending your own position.

Some shows group exhibitors offering similar products together in one area of the hall. A show that served a very high tech industry in its infancy proposed grouping exhibitors by type of product offered. It would be handy, show management thought, for the attendees to go to a certain location and comparison shop. The attendees and the large exhibitors who had distinct product advantages, loved it. Smaller exhibitors with little competitive edge and clout were not pleased and said so but were ignored.

In a year or two as the technological gap decreased, and all exhibitors suffered by easy comparison, even the larger exhibitors clamored about being grouped with the competition. Only then was the scheme done away with.

Usually, show management takes the exact opposite approach in laying out a show. They tend to place exhibitors featuring similar products and services at a distance from each other. It makes the show look more interesting and satisfies the exhibitors, who generally like to be away from the competition.

You should be aware that all space contracts have areas where you can indicate the companies that you do or do not wish to be near. If you are signing up for a show that does not have this space on the application just write a note on any free area of the form.

Step 6: What are the physical aspects of the hall?

Although the physical aspects are not the single biggest factor in selecting space, it can be important to you if you need services like plumbing that are not readily available everywhere in the hall or want to avoid features like columns. The standard physical considerations are the following:

- *Columns.* Can you find a space without them? Or will you need to adjust your exhibit design to accommodate them? Are there columns blocking or changing the traffic flow in the aisles next to your exhibit? Are there columns in the dead space in the back of your exhibit blocking your ability to set up your exhibit easily or store things there?

- *Services.* Which services will you be using and does your location affect their availability? What is the source of the electrical service? Will it be coming from the floor, behind, or overhead, and will that affect the look of your exhibit?

- *Set-up schedule.* Is the hall being set up in stages to allow for a more orderly, less confusing installation? If so, does the time slot designated for your area allow you enough time to set up?

- *Ceiling height.* How tall is your exhibit and does it fit under the ceiling? A West Coast show used the garage to extend the show space, and although the height on the floor plan showed eight feet—the height of most exhibits—exhibitors found that the flooring in the garage was none too even. In some places it was eight feet, but mostly it wasn't.

- *Lighting.* Some halls are dark, some are light. Some use incandescent, some use fluorescent. For example, a grey exhibit might look green in some light and just fine in other light.

Step 7: When will the visitor be the freshest?

Where will visitors be when they are at their freshest? If this is an important factor to you, your exhibit should be somewhere in the middle of the hall, at the crossroads. Space near the center of the hall on a wide cross aisle is highly desirable, because it is seen often as visitors crisscross the hall and are more in the mood to take some time. Here are some other considerations as well:

Big popular exhibits.   When attendees enter the show, they look at the largest exhibits up front and think, "There's a lot to see in that booth so I'll visit them later." Later they are too tired and pass them by thinking, "I know who they are and are aware of their presence in the marketplace, so I haven't missed anything if I skip them."

If yours is a very popular booth and likely to be overcrowded, consider a location that is not so heavily trafficked. The crowds will find you no matter where you are. Overcrowding might sound like a wonderful problem to have but it can actually undermine show goals. Research shows that visitors to an overcrowded booth will identify the staffers as less helpful than those in other exhibits. Even though the overcrowding is not a problem caused by poor staffer behavior, visitors often express it as dissatisfaction with staffers.

Show promoters and show managers often like to have the big name exhibitors in high visibility locations to lend credibility to the show and give the excitement level a boost. If you fall into this category, be sure the front and center location is what you want.

The moods of the attendees changes as the show progresses. When attendees come in the door they usually walk the hall in a casual manner reviewing the show. The exception is shows where there are lots of giveaways, especially if there is a history of running out of them. In this situation, attendees will enter the hall with a fervor that can border on frenzy. Either way, after a casual stroll or a frenzied search for trinkets, within the first hour the crowd settles down to serious sightseeing. By the last hours of the show, the diehards, the late comers, and the real decision makers are the only ones left.

In conclusion, if you use visitor freshness as a factor in space selection, consider locating your exhibit in the middle of the hall.

The following is a quick overview of these seven steps that can organize your thinking about space selection. As you review them, look at the sample floor plans in Fig. 2-1 and think about which spaces you would pick.

Step 1:   Where are the entrance and registration areas?
Step 2:   How will traffic flow from the seminars?
Step 3:   Where are the visitor lounges?
Step 4:   How will traffic flow to and from the facilities (rest rooms and foot service)?
Step 5:   Where is the competition?
Step 6:   What are the physical attributes of the hall? (Columns, availability of services, set-up schedule, ceiling height, lighting.)
Step 7:   When will the visitor by freshest?

What people do at trade shows

The following three tips on how people behave at trade shows can help you fine-tune your space selection methods and give you that extra competitive edge:

1. *They Go Right.* Research shows that about 70 percent of the attendees who come in the main entrance turn right. Operating on the "get them when they're fresh" theory, you will want to pick space a little way back, and slightly to the right side, of the hall.

2. *Odd Aisle.* Exhibit Surveys, Inc., a leading show research firm, has found that, if there are an odd number of aisles, attendees will walk down the next to the last aisle twice. Therefore, exhibitors in that aisle are seen by attendees twice.

3. *People go where other people are.* If attendees hear or see a crowd of people, they are drawn to that crowd. It could be a magician, a presentation, or the best giveaways at the show that draws them. It might even be that all of the largest exhibits and the most popular exhibitors are in one area of the floor. Where there is a crowd of people, expect more to come along.

Finally, if you are thinking about exhibiting in a new show, ask about a discount because the show is unproven. Similarly, if you have a really good speaker that would lend a lot to the conference program, ask for a discount or trade of your speaker for their exhibit space. It never hurts to ask.

3

Budgeting basics

IF YOU'RE LIKE MOST EXHIBITORS, YOU'RE PROBABLY LOOKING FOR A QUICK and easy way to set your trade show budget and eliminate any surprises. You will be spending plenty on exhibiting, and you need to know where your money is going, in advance. By investing only about 15 minutes per show, up-front, you will avoid surprises later—those expenses you either forgot about, or don't know about in advance, like the cost of new graphics, not knowing about drayage, or not planning on substantial deposits sent months in advance.

In this chapter, you'll learn a one-minute calculation for arriving at a budget as well as a simple formula for breaking out specific costs in a rough budget. Last, you'll learn how to fine-tune your own zero-based budget using a spreadsheet to integrate it into a month-by-month, departmental operating budget of forecasted expenses.

Portable vs. custom exhibit

Budgeting is very different for portable exhibits than for custom exhibits. Custom exhibits are designed and built just for you. They are constructed of heavy materials, shipped in heavy, durable crates, and require laborers to set them up. The weight increases both shipping and drayage costs—the service of taking your exhibitry from one location to the other in the show hall, and their complex designs make each set-up different and, compared with porta-

32

ble exhibits, costly. But that is the higher price you pay for a unique display that has impact.

By contrast, portable exhibits are manufactured, are lighter in weight, and are meant to be easily set up by one person, usually in less than an hour. If you are using a portable exhibit, you can carry it to the show yourself and set it up yourself, thus eliminating the need for transportation, drayage, and set-up labor charges. You will not, however, have a totally unique exhibit.

As you can see, it's a trade off. The high price of a custom exhibit should net the greater impact because of its unique design, whereas the portable exhibit is economic, but its design (impact) is limited. These differences will have significant impact on the budgeting process. Therefore, as you go through this chapter, you will find that each part addresses the expenses and budgeting methods associated with first the portable exhibit and then the custom exhibit. If you already know what type of exhibit you want, you might want to go immediately to the part that applies to you.

Calculating a ballpark budget

There are three steps you can use to arrive at a budget for any show on your schedule:

1. Calculate the total budget.
2. Divide the budget into expense categories.
3. Build a detailed show budget using a zero-based budget method.

Let's begin with step one and a simple calculation for arriving at your total budget. There are two useful formulas you will want to keep at your fingertips:

1. Portable exhibit: 3 x the cost of exhibit space
2. Custom exhibit: 4 x the cost of exhibit space

This method is fast, and it is just what you need anytime you want to know the total cost of exhibiting quickly.

Suppose, for example, your boss or sales manager suggests exhibiting at a show he or she needs to have a ballpark budget fast. There is a catch, however. When you use this formula, you don't know how much will be spent on individual aspects of exhibiting, like transportation, drayage, or refurbishment of the exhibit. You won't know about them until you think about each one individually, and that can't be done with a formula such as this. On the other hand, if you just need a rough estimate of what the show is going to cost in total, then this method is fine.

Calculating how the total budget will be spent

Now that you have a total budget, the next step is to break it down by category of expense. If you have experience with show budgeting and are comfortable working without guidelines, you can go directly to the zero-based budget and begin calculating precisely how you intend to spend that total budget pie. Otherwise, make this interim stop and roughly carve up the total cost you arrived at using standard percent allocations.

Table 3-1 shows a rough allocation of expenses for a portable exhibit and Table 3-2 shows the same for a custom exhibit. Keep in mind that these numbers are only averages and that your individual situation could be quite different. Take a hard look at them and then think about how you spend money on exhibiting.

While this is an easy way to carve out a rough budget, always remember that they are representational only of what other people do. You might have a history of, and a very good reason for, doing otherwise. The best possible route is to keep your own history of expenses and calculate your own percentages. This way, you'll be confident that your rough budget is very close to the real thing.

Using zero-based budgeting

The best method of budgeting is zero-based budgeting because it provides you a thorough picture of exactly where you will be spending your dollars. As with any other zero-based budget, you simply identify all of the budget elements and estimate them. It is the safest way to set a budget because of the discipline of the process. In order for zero-based to really work for you, each line item should be justified. That is, for each item you place into the budget, you should be able to justify that expense.

Table 3-1.
Rough Budget for Portable Exhibits

Expenses	Percent
Exhibit space	33
Refurbishment	8
Transportation	6
Show services	5
Personnel	19
Specialty advertising items	10
Miscellaneous	18

Research provided by Skyline Displays, Inc., Burnsville, MN.

_____ **Table 3-2.** _____
Rough Budget for Custom Exhibits

Expenses	Percent
Exhibit space	24
Exhibit construction costs prorated	23
Refurbishment	10
Transportation	13
Show services	22
Personnel	2
Specialty advertising	2
Miscellaneous	4

Source: The Trade Show Bureau Research Report on Cost analysis, #2060, August 1988.

As you can see, zero-based budgeting eliminates surprises in two important ways. First, the detailed work involved in thinking through all of the line items will uncover otherwise "hidden," or forgotten expenses. Second, every line item will be justified, thereby eliminating unneeded expenses. By taking the time to do a zero-based budget, you ensure that your trade show dollars are being spent wisely.

Take a quick glance at the zero-based budget chart in Fig. 3-1 for portable exhibits and Fig. 3-2 for custom exhibits. Most of it is easy, but here are a few pointers to help you along. As you read, you might have specific questions about how each of these services works and they will be covered in Chapters 4 and 5. Here we are concerned only with cost implications.

Portable exhibit budgeting tips

Use of a portable, or manufactured, exhibit greatly simplifies the zero-based budgeting process. Many of the line items can be greatly reduced or even eliminated. The following are four pointers for budgeting when using a portable exhibit:

Transportation.   If saving money is your aim, then carry what you can, ship anything that is small enough to the hotel, and send only the largest, heaviest and bulkiest items by common carrier. This will eliminate or reduce the need for transportation and drayage charges.

If, on the other hand, you desire the utmost in convenience, then send everything to the hall. In this case, you will get a drayage bill, but your shipment will be brought right to your booth space and you won't have to lift a finger. If you go this route, be sure to send all boxes and crates in one shipment, not separately. There is a minimum drayage charge for each shipment and, therefore, small packages left to the last minute will be billed at

The exhibit
  actual cost or amount amortized   _____
  new graphics, etc.   _____

Transportation
  early shipments   _____
  last minute (air freight)   _____

Services at the show
  drayage   _____
  set up and dismantle labor   _____
    hourly rate $_____ × no. of hrs.   _____
  electrical   _____
  cleaning   _____
  rental (furniture, etc.)   _____
  florist   _____
  phone   _____
  other utilities (water, etc.)   _____
  security   _____
Promotions
  pre-show promotions   _____
  at-show promotions   _____
Personnel
  at-show promotions   _____
Personnel
  travel   _____
  hotel   _____
                    Total   _____

Fig. 3-1. A portable exhibit zero-based budget.

that minimum charge, which makes delivery more expensive than if it had been shipped with everything else.

Drayage. In some halls, the draymen must carry the portable exhibit to the exhibitor's booth space, while in others, the exhibitor can carry, or more likely, wheel, it in himself. Some halls say carrying is fine, but the use of wheeled carts is not. If you plan to wheel in your portable, be sure you know the prevailing policy. Check the exhibitors kit or call the show manager.

Labor. As will be discussed in the next chapter, you have the right to set up the exhibit yourself if it can be done without tools and in under 30 minutes. Most portable exhibits fall under this definition, so you will probably set the exhibit up yourself and save substantially on labor charges.

Other services. If you are using a portable exhibit or have a small space with any type of exhibit, you might not need phone service or security. Take a moment now to review the budget work sheet in Fig. 3-2.

The exhibit
   actual cost or amount amortized   _____
   new graphics, etc.   _____

Transportation
   early shipments*   _____
   last minute (air freight)*   _____

Services at the show
   drayage*   _____
   set up and dismantle labor*   _____
     hourly rate $_____ × no. of hrs.   _____
   electrical   _____
   cleaning*   _____
   rental (furniture, etc.)   _____
   florist*   _____
   phone*   _____
   other utilities (water, etc.)*   _____
   security*   _____

Promotions   _____
   pre-show promotions   _____
   travel   _____
   hotel   _____
                       Total   _____

*Might not apply when you are using a portable exhibit.

Fig. 3-2. A custom exhibit zero-based budget.

Custom exhibit budgeting tips

The following are five tips for budgeting when using a custom exhibit:

The exhibit property.   Think about whether you will need repairs or graphics used just at one or a couple of shows. The cost of a new exhibit that will be used over many years is often amortized, which is discussed later in this chapter.

Transportation.   Your next cost decision concerns transportation and how you plan to get the exhibit, literature, and anything else that you will need to the show. You can take some things with you. For example, a few boxes of literature can be checked as baggage or put in the trunk of your car. Last minute packages, if small, can be shipped via any of the parcel services, such as UPS, or if they are very last minute, air freight.

If you can't take it with you, and it's too big or heavy for UPS, then you will probably need to send the rest of it by common carrier or van line. Each has advantages, which are explained in Chapter 4 on planning logistics. Keep in mind that the ability to send exhibitry pad wrapped, via van line, has repercussions in higher costs. Van lines tend to be more expensive. Additionally, your drayage bill will be higher because goods that are uncrated are billed with a surcharge of 50 to 100 percent. It might be tempting to use pad wrapping, thus eliminating the need for crating, which can offer quite a savings, just remember that it will cost you more in drayage charges. You will need drayage to get your things from the loading dock to the booth space or from the door of the hall to the booth space.

Services.   If you are not sure or have no experience estimating how much it will cost to set up your exhibit, call your exhibit supplier for a realistic estimate. They will let you know how long it will take to set up your exhibit, and you can just look up the hourly rate for labor in the exhibitors kit. Exhibitor kits are sent once you sign up. In the mean time, just call the show manager and ask about the hourly rate for labor.

Other services.   You might need cleaning and vacuuming of the exhibit, electrical service for lighting or equipment, furniture rental, carpet rental, floral arrangements, phone, and security. Most of these costs can easily be estimated by looking at the exhibitor kit for the show you are attending. If you really want to be an expert at estimating all of these items, just look at, and compare, a couple of exhibitor kits.

You might not need everything listed on this budget work sheet in Fig. 3-3 but it should start your thinking process.

Handling exhibit property expense

The purchase of a new exhibit is often a capital acquisition and, as such, requires special financial consideration.

If you have purchased a portable exhibit under $10,000, you can "expense" it, or write it off, in that year as you would with any other capital equipment purchase. Any capital purchase more than $10,000, which would include some large or elaborate portable exhibits and most custom exhibits, are usually depreciated over the usable life of the exhibit. Consult your accountant to determine the proper handling of exhibit cost amortization. Each exhibit property should be adequately insured. The liability of your transportation provider and exhibit house will be limited and you must purchase insurance to make up the difference.

Pulling it all together

Up till now, we have been looking at budgets for just one show. It's time to pull it all together into an annual budget for your trade show program so that you end up with a "spreadsheet" of monthly, forecasted expenses. (See Fig. 3-3). This way, you will be able to see where the money is going on a monthly basis, when during the year expenses will take place, as well as the total price tag on the program.

In realistically evaluating the cost of your trade show program, be sure

Chart of Accounts	Jan	Feb	Mar	Apr	May	Jun	Jul	Aug	Sept*	Oct	Nov	Dec	TOTAL
Space			1,800.00										1,800.00
Services						150.00		875.00	140.00				1,165.00
Transportation										1,200.00			1,200.00
Exhibit													
—New Graphics						1,500.00		1,500.00					3,000.00
Amortization									2,800.00				2,800.00
Personnel										7,500.00	1,200.00		8,700.00
—travel													
Totals			1,800.00			1,650.00		2,375.00	2,940.00	8,700.00	1,200.00		18,665.00

*Denotes show month

1. Second half of space cost deposit, paid six months out.
2. Show service deposits and pre-payments paid prior to the show.
2a. Payment of services at the show by credit card.
3. Transportation invoice paid one month after show.
4. Graphics paid 50 percent with order, balance on delivery.
5. Portion of original purchase price allocated to this show usage. This is only one way to show this. It could also be included as departmental overhead or as a regular monthly posting to its own line item.
6. Travel expense reports usually arrive three to eight weeks after the show. Personnel travel expenses may or may not come from the trade show budget.

Fig. 3-3. A typical spreadsheet forecast of monthly expenses for one show. The annual show budget is simply a compilation of all the show budgets.

to look for "hidden costs" like personnel time and benefits, lost opportunity costs because your sales staff is at the show and not out in the field, local mailings paid for by the local sales office, and so on. Only then will you be able to know what it's costing you to exhibit and be able to evaluate whether or not you are getting a return for that investment.

4

Organizing show services

EVERY EXHIBITOR NEEDS TO KNOW AS MUCH AS POSSIBLE ABOUT SETUP AND services because, other than the cost of building the exhibit, these are the largest expenses. If you ever hope to exhibit at a reasonable cost, you must become knowledgeable about logistics. Then too, if someone who reports to you takes care of all of the details, you need to know where they are spending the money and why. If this is your situation, and your inclination is to spend the least amount of time on this topic as possible, consider thoroughly reading this chapter then skimming over the next one, which covers managing setup on the show floor.

Setup attitudes

It's a safe bet that all exhibitors have had a negative attitude about setup at one time or other. Some dislike or are afraid of it. Some think that it's boring, while others are sure they are going to be ripped off. In fact, exhibitors with negative attitudes do become victims of this self-fulfilling prophecy, and 40 percent of all first-time exhibitors never exhibit again. But this can be avoided.

Typically, exhibitors have the most problems during setup when they don't understand what's happening on the show floor, haven't done any planning, and let their poor attitude get in the way. If this describes you, then you really need this chapter. It can help you understand the chain of command, who to go to for help, and how to plan your setup so that it is just about hassle free.

While there is much activity on the show floor, it is not designed solely to make your life miserable. In fact, there is a system in place that works very well and should work well for you also. This system enables tons of goods and materials to enter the hall and be built into stunning displays in a very few days. In order to do that, things must happen fast and on a tight schedule.

If you have an understanding of how everything works and a plan in place, your job during setup is easily distilled to simply waiting for events to go astray from your plan and managing them when they do. This allows you to relax and enjoy the scenery—the action of setup—without the anxiety.

In this chapter, we will consider the paperwork: the space contract and the exhibitors manual or kit and its service order forms. In the next chapter, we will go on to examine what happens on the show floor, including all of the players, scheduling, and the "how-to's" of getting your exhibit up on time.

A portable exhibit case study

The following is a case study of a portable exhibit setup, in diary form, that will show you why good planning is the entire key to saving time and money. The exhibitor is using a portable exhibit in their 10 by 10-foot booth space.

Saturday, PM: Arrive on afternoon flight. The exhibit consisting of two cases plus a box of product samples, was checked as luggage. Upon arrival at hotel, check with bell desk for two boxes containing our literature, shipped via UPS, second day, last week. They tell me to check with the business office. Business office is closed and won't re-open until 8:30 Monday, and the show opens at 10:00. Must remember to pick them up Monday or we'll have nothing to hand out. Get to sleep early, tomorrow could be a long day.

Sunday, 9:30 AM: Leave the box of product samples in my room and wheel the two cases containing the exhibit over to the hall, across the street. Guard at the door won't let me in without a badge. Go get the badge.

Guard won't let me in with a wheeled cart. Says I can only carry things in, otherwise it must be taken around to the loading dock and given to the people in drayage. I disassemble the cart and carry in both cases.

A little exhausted, am cheered up when I see that the rental carpet, four chairs, smoke stand and two tables are already in the booth. On closer look, this is not my booth. I'm in the wrong aisle.

Now in the correct booth, my rental carpet, etc. is also in place. Start to set up the display, but with all the rental furniture, there is no room. Maybe I've ordered too much furniture. Move some out.

10:45 AM: Try to plug in the header lights. No electrical service. Forgot to order it. Go to service desk and do so. It's going to cost a whole lot more than it would have if I had remembered about the lights and ordered it two weeks ago. Woman behind the desk asks how I would like to pay. Can they bill me? No, we don't have an account. She tells me they take major credit cards and traveler's checks. Didn't bring traveler's checks, so give her my Visa card.

Look around at the other service desks to see what else I might have overlooked. Plants, photography? Don't need them. Imprinter? Ordered it, so might as well pick it up now. Use my badge card to check the imprinter. Have to go through four before I find one that gives a dark impression that can easily be read.

12:00 Noon: No electrician. Check back at the desk and am told that they can't get to me until late afternoon. The orders from all of the exhibitors who ordered prior to the show are before my order.

Since I'm back at the service desk, I check the order for cleaning. No problem there, and they will vacuum early tomorrow before the show opens. Go to lunch and back to the hotel to pick up the box of product samples.

1:30 PM: Check back at the booth and find that the electrician has come and left. The header is lit up. Move about half of the rental furniture back into the booth. One table and two chairs is plenty. Visit the furniture rental desk and try to get them to change the order and get a credit for what we don't need. Payment was sent with the order so I need a refund. No one seems to know how to do that. The person who can issue a refund will be back at 2:30.

2:30 PM: The rental refund person is not back yet. Come back later. Have time to kill, so leisurely tidy up the booth. Lay out product samples and store empty boxes and exhibit cases under draped table.

3:00 PM: Check back at rental desk. Person who can help me was there but went back to the office. Will be back tomorrow. They tell me to leave my name and booth number and they will find me tomorrow morning. Go back to hotel. Feel like I've walked about 75 miles.

Monday, 8:30 AM: Check in hotel business office for boxes and find them right away. Am luckier than the guy standing next to me who has been looking for something sent to the hotel since Friday. Luckily, I ran into an associate who helps me with boxes, otherwise I'd have to use the wheeled cart again and that would cause problems at the door.

"We arrive at the exhibit, which has been vacuumed. All the product samples are gone. I double check. Sure enough, they have been stolen. Well, at least we have the literature.

I find a note in the booth from the furniture rental people that the refund has been taken care of and they will drop off a check later.

10:30 AM: The show opens and we are ready. Call the office and tell them to ship another box of product samples overnight.

Had this exhibitor been more knowledgeable and done better planning, his setup would have run more smoothly, and he would have saved money. Let's review what happened and how it could have gone a lot better.

The exhibitor should have checked to make sure the literature had arrived before leaving the hotel. In that phone call, he would have found out that all packages for guests are kept in the business office. Business offices are often open just during the week. By waiting until he was on site and just an hour and a half before the opening of the show, he left no margin for error.

The incident with the wheeled cart not being let into the hall is typical of large halls with strict union jurisdictions. This exhibitor did the sensible thing and just took everything off the cart and carried in what he could. If he would have had too much to carry in, he could have used a drayman to assist. The guard's admonition that his only alternative was to wheel the cart outside and all the way around to the back was a little stiff. But here is the dilemma with which the exhibitor is faced. He needs to go get a drayman, but he can't go into the hall with his things to get one. Should he leave them alone at the guard's station? Would this particular guard be flexible enough to allow him to do so? A phone call to the show manager in the planning phase would have prevented confusion at the door.

Our exhibitor wasn't very organized about his service order forms. He had no documentation with him and was not clear about what he had ordered or what he needed. Therefore, his on-site order for electrical service cost him a premium as well as a delay. While his delay was not crucial to his set-up schedule because his exhibit was simple, it might have been.

This exhibitor had not checked the exhibitors manual to find out about payment policies, nor had he thought about how he was going to pay for any services purchased on site. If he had, he might have wanted to bring traveler's checks.

The product samples, and anything of value, should not be put out until just before the show opens.

As you read the rest of this chapter, think of how the setups you've handled might have been easier had you planned better.

Understanding exhibit space contracts

The first step towards exhibiting at a particular show happens when you sign the space contract. Practically speaking, if you only go to one or two shows a year, and you need to be there, you have probably signed contracts without giving them a second look. Certainly, everyone should be careful about signing contracts without reading them, but when exhibitors need to be in a show, they sign willingly. You give them money; they give you space. The question is, what space, where, and when, encumbered by what restrictions and with which rights. The contract will tell you precisely what you are buying. Some of the things that can be found on a typical contract for exhibit space are:

- *Date and place of the event.*
- *Hours of the show.*
- *Who is eligible to exhibit.* There could be restrictions on eligibility that would prevent a jewelry distributor from selling gold chains at a high tech or health care event.
- *Type of products to be shown.* Limitations of all sorts are found here, but most often exhibitors are limited to displaying those products and services that are of interest to this particular audience. Usually applies only to business-to-business shows.
- *Restrictions on subletting.* The booth space, or a portion of it, cannot be sublet.
- *Payment and cancellation deadlines and penalties.*
- *Standard booth equipment.* Some shows will include at no extra charge at least some of the following: sign, carpet, minimal electrical outlets, chairs, waste baskets and smoking stands. Check during setup to make sure you are getting all that you paid for.
- *Display rules.* Maximum height, unfinished sides of the display, obstruction of view of adjacent displays, lighting, and sound limitations.
- *Traffic-building techniques and giveaways.* Wide variety of restrictions here. Read each contract to note limitations on contests, drawings, giveaways, models in costumes, and literature. Often, these have to be approved by show management.
- *Fire regulations.* All display materials must be flameproof. Any materials you are using in the display that are not flameproof should be sprayed with a fire retardant, which most exhibit houses can do.
- *Hours of installation and dismantling.*
- *Union labor and use of nonofficial contractors.* In this section, you consent to abide by agreements and jurisdictions set up by the show facility and the local unions. This often means that you agree to use union labor. The paragraphs that deal with non-official contractors range widely, from simply informing show management that you will be using a non-official contractor to set up your exhibit, to limiting or disallowing the use of non-official contractors at all. Non-officials will always have to present a certificate of insurance.
- *Liability.* Who is liable for accidents in your exhibit and elsewhere on the show floor.
- *Cancellation of the event.* Who owes whom if the show is cancelled.

All of these can be important to your planning, and so it's wise to grab a cup of strong coffee and read the contract thoroughly before signing it.

Exhibitors kit: dream or nightmare?

Not reading the contract might cost you money, but not thoroughly reading the exhibitors kit is certain to cost you money. It contains the forms for ordering services and advisories on other information, such as hours of set up, deadlines, and the like. The better manuals are a dream and will be in a three-ring binder and include an array of very useful information, like where the show office can be found, lists of press people who have been invited to the show, date schedule checklists and other "how-to" information. (See Figs. 4-1 and 4-2 for sample exhibitor kits.)

At the least, you should expect to see a manual that is well organized and neat. Some are a nightmare of poorly copied, not quite legible, service forms. You can tell a lot about the organizational skills of the show manager and how setup is likely to be handled by the orderliness of the exhibitors manual. If the kit is orderly, setup is usually orderly.

There are two parts to a manual, although you might not find it divided

Fig. 4-1. Two typical exhibitor kits.

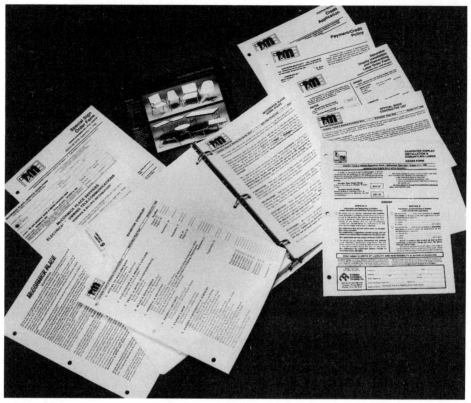

Fig. 4-2. Contents of an excellent exhibitor kit.

that way. They are: general information that instructs and informs and contractor information about show services. Figure 4-3 is a list of what you might find in each. As you can see, very valuable information can be found in the exhibitor manual, if you will only take the time to read it and do a little work. One of the important tasks you need to do right away is scheduling.

Creating a schedule

One of the most useful items a show manager can provide for you is a schedule of important dates. If you don't find one, usually in the very front of the exhibitor kit, you need to make one. Only by using it will you feel secure about meeting all important due dates.

Each service order form will have a due date on it somewhere. The objective here is to get those dates into some chronology. This doesn't have to be a time-consuming job. Just grab a sheet of paper and as you go through the manual, jot down the important dates. In addition to show service order

General Information	Contractor Information
Cover letter	Forms for:
Table of contents	booth cleaning
Hours:	carpet rental
registration	furniture
show	signage
move in/out	labor order
seminars	rigger order
Show office location	electrical order
Badges	gas order
Contacts:	food service
show management	phone
facility	audio/visual
contractors	security
Message center	floral
Exhibitor meeting	photography
Promotion plans for the show	Customized services
Press services:	Payment instructions
press room	Credit applications
press conference	Shipping forms/labels
Show directory	Labor rules
Exhibitor registration	Proof of insurance
Hotel information	Service desk locations
Parking	Deadlines for service order
Transportation	
Latest floor plan	
List of exhibitors and booth number	
Fire regulations	
Security regulations	
removal pass policy	

Fig. 4-3. Exhibitor kit contents list.

deadlines, you will need to add shipping dates, exhibit construction milestones and other important dates.

If you do just one or two shows a year, a schedule/checklist identifying all of the due dates is probably good enough, provided you remember to look at it periodically. If you take care of many shows, you are better off with a calendar that displays deadlines for all of the shows at once. Try writing in due dates on one of those big wall calendars from the office supply store. If you like computers, you might want to get some project management software and adjust it for handling shows.

No matter how you do it, you must use a schedule of some sort. Missed deadlines translate into extra money because services cost more when ordered at the show. Figure 4-4 shows a simple schedule/checklist that could be used for each show. Just remember, once you get three or four of these going at once, you will probably need a master calendar on the wall or on a computer.

Schedule/Checklist

Show _____

Date _____

Booth # _____

	A	B	C	D	E	F	G
1	Item	Due	Ck#	Po#	Vendor	Forecast	Actual
2	Space Contract						
3	Exhibit Maintenance						
4	—New Graphics						
5							
6	Show Services						
7	—Transportation						
8	—Drayage						
9	—Setup/Dismantle Labor						
10	—Riggers						
11	—Plant Rental						
12	—Telephone						
13	—Cleaning						
14	—Electrical						
15	—Hostesses						
16	—Smokers/Waste						
17	—Plumbing						
18	—Photographer						
19	—Audio/Visual						
20	—Pre-Show Training						
21	—Show Research						
22	—Lead Forms						
23							
24	Staff Needs:						
25	Travel Arrangements						
26	—Hotel						
27	—Air/Auto						
28	Show Registration						
29	Custom Name Badges						
30							
31	Miscellaneous						
32	—Show Literature						
33	—Give-aways						
34	—Pre-Show Mailing						
35	—Press Kits						
36	—Post-Show Mailings						
37							
38	Other						
39	—						
40	—						

Fig. 4-4. Sample schedule.

Creating a site book

One of the most useful tools you can easily make for yourself is a site book. It is just a three-ring binder that contains a copy of any pertinent paperwork, which you take with you to set up. (Never take original paperwork out of the office because it could get lost.)

The three-ring binder ensures that when you drop it while juggling a briefcase, your glasses, the set-up drawings, and a box of wing nut bolts, the papers won't scatter. To assemble the site book, just make two copies of every service order form, or any other important paperwork, and put one in the book when you put one in the file.

Tips on documentation

The following are two helpful hints that can make things run better. The first is about making notes on every phone conversation you have with show personnel and taking those notes with you in the site book. You know how it is anytime you're trying to get a project underway, you talk to someone who says, yes they can, and the next person you talk to says, no, they never do that, and wants to know who told you that you could, but you don't have the first person's name. When talking to anyone, get their name and make a notation in the site book of the time, date, and what was said. It could come in handy later.

This second tip is especially important if you work in a larger company where deposit checks are likely to be sent out from the accounts payable department. Make a note on the check request form that you want the check returned to you, not sent to the supplier. This way, you can make a copy of it for the site book. Consider sending it return receipt requested just in case you need to prove that the check was received.

Getting organized

If you coordinate a number of shows and find that you are always rummaging through the files to locate the same information, this tip is for you. Use a five-by-eight-inch index card for each show filled with often-used information. This way, the right data is at your fingertips fast when you need it, and you don't have to go digging through the files for answers.

A woman who handles over 200 shows a year uses this system, and on the phone, she sounds like a genius with total recall and the best memory in the business.

Service order forms

The trick to service order forms is getting them in on time. Most forms are easy to fill out and won't present a problem for you. Just be aware of the deadlines, which should go on your calendar as discussed earlier in the chapter.

Why are deadlines so important? Think about it from the contractors point of view. Imagine for a moment that you are the one responsible for getting electrical service to 500 booths, you only have two days to do it, and all of them need something different. Wouldn't you want to have those service order forms in as soon as possible? Looking at it this way, it's easy to see why all services cost less when ordered ahead of time.

If you miss the deadline and have to order at the show, not only will it cost you more for the exact same service, but your request will probably be put at the end of the line. Some exhibitors ignore deadlines, order at the show, then try to circumvent the system by tipping to be moved up in line. Depending on the show, they might be taken care of faster, although that is far from guaranteed, but they could have saved their gratuity and the surcharge and gotten the same results by getting the service forms in on time.

It is also a good idea to call about two weeks prior to the show to check that all of the orders were received and that there are no problems. Here is a quick review of services with some pointers on how to order them.

Labor

You always have the right to set up your own exhibit, provided one person can do it without tools in less than a half hour. This is why portable exhibits are so popular, especially those that just pop up. If you cannot set it up yourself, you will need laborers.

In most halls, the labor that you are ordering is union labor. Each union has jurisdiction over specific types of work done on the show floor. For instance, in Chicago, the Carpenters Union takes care of setup, while the Teamsters Union handles drayage. The exhibitors manual should make it clear which services need to be ordered from which union. If it is not clear, just call the show manager's office.

Remember, unless it states otherwise in the contract, you can hire your own laborers and/or a supervisor to work with them. More about this in the next chapter.

Drayage

Drayage is the service of moving your exhibit and other freight from the loading dock to your booth space. Understand that getting all of the freight to all of the exhibits is a monumental task. Everybody wants it *now*. Most exhibitors feel that drayage is very expensive, however. It is billed on the hundred weight, or CWT, that is, each hundred pounds of your freight will cost you so many dollars.

It is important for you to know and be able to document the weight of your freight, because that's how you are billed. Documentation is the key, because if you are not able to prove the weight of your exhibitry, they have the right to weigh it themselves. Ask your exhibit supplier or your transportation carrier for a weight ticket and check your drayage bills against it.

Usually, you are simply billed the same drayage amount for entry as for removal. If, however, you are giving out plenty of literature and give-aways at the show, say a couple of hundred pounds of it, then you will want to note that on your drayage order form and double check this on site to ensure that your outbound drayage bill is appropriately less than the inbound bill.

Any freight that is not crated or boxed is billed at a premium rate, usually a 50 percent, or even a 100 percent surcharge. Some exhibitors with large custom exhibits will save on the cost of building crates and pad wrap their exhibits. (If you are not familiar with this, the next time you are at a show setup, look around during the early part of setup for moving pads or blankets.) These pads should be put on with straps or strapping tape, but often, you will see them half falling off because someone used masking tape, which is not strong enough.

Pads cause the draymen problems because they are messy and not of uniform shape, making them harder to handle than materials in crates, which are of a uniform size. That's why pad wrapped or mixed shipments are billed at a surcharge.

Electrical

Ordering electrical service is easy. All you have to do is find out how much power is needed by: 1) the exhibitry and 2) the equipment on display. Your exhibit house can tell you about the exhibitry and your audio/visual supplier, and your company's technical people can tell you about the equipment in the exhibit. This will give you the volts and watts and/or amps.

Once you know your requirements, and if you are still confused, simply call the electrical contractor. Some kind person will guide you through their form and clear up any problems. Don't feel ill at ease if you don't understand it all. Just ask. The electrical contractor wants you to get it right, and they are happy to spend a few minutes with you on the phone, thereby avoiding any confusion on the show floor. You, naturally, don't want to cause problems for yourself during setup by having to arrange for more electrical service because you didn't order enough. You also don't want to waste money by ordering too much. Instead, just call them.

Cleaning

If your exhibit is small, you will probably want to order one cleaning, or more specifically, vacuuming, scheduled for opening day of the show. This ensures that all of the mess created by setup has been removed and that the booth looks good for the opening of the show. On the other days of the show, you can save money and pick up the big pieces of dirt and lint by hand.

Instead of ordering cleaning services, you can always bring your own vacuum cleaner and sweep the carpet yourself. This is not an activity over which any union has jurisdiction. For most exhibitors, that's a job they don't want to do, so they order cleaning services.

Large, impressive exhibits can get much of their overall look from expanses of colorful carpet, and so how the carpet looks is important. Here, it is wise to order a daily cleaning service.

Every exhibit needs a "wipe down" to eliminate dust and dirt before it looks it's best. You will probably want to keep a roll of paper towels and some all purpose cleaner around for touch-up.

Furniture

You will need some furniture for your exhibit area. The following is a list of some common furniture you might need:

- *Waste basket* If it won't be seen, use a box you don't need for return shipment or a garbage bag brought from the home or office.

- *Smoking stand* Smoking stands encourage staffers to smoke in the exhibit and they should not be smoking there. You can do without one.

- *Chairs* Chairs encourage staffers to sit, and they should spend their time standing and talking to visitors. However, if you need chairs in a lounge area for visitors or for a conference room—don't forget to order a conference table—then it will cost you less to rent them at each show rather than to buy and ship them from show to show.

- *The exhibit* You can rent an exhibit. This can be done either through an official contractor, your own exhibit house, or an exhibit supplier who specializes in rental exhibits.

- *Carpet* Some exhibitors, mostly larger ones who want to enhance the look of the exhibit by having the color of the carpet exactly match a certain shade used elsewhere in the exhibit, bring their own carpet. The rest rent theirs. If you don't like the selections offered by the official contractor, there are firms that specialize in carpet rental. Their selections are usually of a better grade and come in a wide variety of colors and styles. They cost more too. Your exhibit house should be able to put you in contact with them.

If you want to protect your carpeting during setup, order Visqueen, a clear plastic, with your carpet order.

Floral arrangements and plants

Flowers and plants certainly can brighten up an exhibit. If you have the time and energy, and if saving costs is important, shop for plants at discount stores, supermarkets, and garden centers in the show town and bring them into the exhibit yourself, especially if you only need a couple of ferns and some cut flowers. You can save by buying them outside of the hall. If convenience is your priority, then order them from the show florist. Silk plants can also be a reusable alternative.

Photography

It is very useful to keep a photo album of what your exhibit looks like at the various shows you attend. It is a great help during planning. One print should be packed with the exhibit so that the laborers can see what the assembled display will look like.

If you are a competent photographer, and remembered to bring your camera, you might want to save money by taking the pictures yourself instead of using the official show photographers. If you decide to use a show photographer, just keep in mind that it can be costly.

Security

You need security whenever you are not able to remove or lock up at the end of the day any valuables that are on display. No exhibitor is exempt. One manufacturer of locks had all of their locks stolen. What should be secured? The list would include popular computer, consumer electronics, or audio/visual equipment or anything that could be used in the home.

Understand that having a guard on duty is not always a deterrent. One exhibitor came in the next morning to find that the guard he hired was asleep and his valuables were missing.

In addition to reputable security firms, try local, off-duty law enforcement officers. They know the local characters and take security seriously.

Telephone/telecommunications

Save money and don't order a phone for the staffers to use. If you must have a phone in the booth, put a lock on it so that it can only be used for incoming calls. That way staffers won't spend most of their time on the phone when they should be talking to visitors.

Don't forget to lock up the phones and jacks overnight to prevent unauthorized calls. One exhibit forgot to do that and found $400 worth of calls to Venezuela on the bill. Many exhibitors are eliminating these problems by using cellular phones that can be rented.

Audio/visual

If you rent any audio or visual equipment, check to see who is responsible for it overnight. You might need to find a secure place to store it.

Signage

If you want a hand-painted sign, you can order it from your local signmaker and possibly save money. If you need something made up at the last minute, the official signmaker can make one for you on site.

Imprinters and lead forms

Some shows register attendees and give them paper badges while others use plastic credit card-type badges. Credit card imprinters can capture the information on the card. Imprinters can be rented. Just buy a pack of imprinter forms. The problem with lead forms is that they greatly limit the amount of information you can put on them. What you need is a custom form, which you will find out more about in chapter 6.

When you pick up the imprinter, use your own credit card-type badge to check the quality of the imprint. Run off a form or two to make sure the imprinter gives a good, clear impression. The service desk people might hand you their own cards with which to test the imprinter. Sometimes these cards have been bent to give the best impression. Use your own card.

Models/hostesses

Renting a chair is not an issue of great magnitude. Renting a person is, because they represent you to your visitors. It will be worth it to take the extra time to call around to other exhibitors for recommendations on the best temporary help agencies. Be certain that you check the agencies references and that you are very specific about the type of person you need. Be sure to request that they have trade show experience.

If you want someone in business attire, prefer a male or female, or someone with specific secretarial abilities, you'll need to let the agency know. If you get on site and the model or host/hostess is not all you had wished for, just speak up and get a replacement.

Transportation

How are you going to get your exhibit and other materials to the show? If you are attending a local event with a portable exhibit, you might just put the display in the trunk of the car and unload it at the front door of the hall.

If you are using a portable exhibit and flying to the show, you might opt to check it as baggage. Most exhibitors who check it use curbside check in and tip the skycap generously, thereby avoiding any hassle with the agents inside.

Your portable exhibit, as well as any last-minute packages, can also be sent UPS or by other similar carriers. If you are not sending large, heavy, or numerous packages, so as to create a problem getting them from the hotel to the hall, consider sending your materials to the hotel where there will be far fewer packages arriving.

If your small shipment gets sent to the hall, it will be handled by drayage, and you will be charged for it. If you can carry it into the hall yourself—and in some halls that means no wheeled carts—you will avoid drayage charges. If you are sending all of your freight to the hall, send it as one shipment so you will incur only one drayage bill and one minimum charge.

Be aware that many parcel delivery services will pick up from hotels and halls alike, but you will only be able to issue a pick up order to a hotel. If your package is picked up from the hall, there will be a drayage charge. Remember that UPS and other delivery services have size limitations. Call your carrier for specifics.

You can also send exhibitry air freight, but there are size limitations. The advantage is that you get it there fast; the disadvantage is that you pay for that luxury. If you find that you are waiting until the last minute and sending everything by air freight, you could save substantially by being better organized.

For custom exhibitry and large products, your two choices are common carrier and van line. If your exhibit program is large enough to need these services, shop carefully because you will save money. If you have a corporate traffic department, enlist their help to get the best rates.

A word here about an ethics issue—kickbacks. In a very large exhibits program there are two large expense areas that lend themselves to kickbacks. One is transportation. The other you will have to read the rest of the book to find out. If you manage someone who manages a large amount of transportation, make certain that you are very involved with the bidding process and all negotiations.

If you are the person who selects the transportation provider and you are offered a kickback, don't take it. If you are caught, it could ruin your career.

How do you decide between using common carrier and van line? Simply put, if you have delicate exhibitry, exhibitry that's pad wrapped and not in crates, or delicate product, then you will want to consider van line. If you have a very tight and precise setup schedule, then van line is the way to go. If you like having a transportation provider representative on the show floor to give you a moment-by-moment account of the arrival of your shipment, then go with a van line that provides that service.

Common carrier is for you if economy is a high priority and all of your exhibitry is in crates or boxes. Just about as many exhibitors use common carrier as use van line.

If arranging for freight is something that you don't want to be bothered with, ask your exhibit house or your independent installation and dismantle firm to take care of it for you. They will either charge you a fee, which usually comes to about 20 percent of the transportation bill, or take a finders fee from the transportation provider. This is an earned administration fee and they are entitled to it, even though some aren't very quick to point it out to their clients.

Once you have decided on how you will send your exhibitry, you need to keep a crate contents list for each crate and number them. This will also help you direct draymen where things should be set the *first* time, which saves you time (and that means money) at the setup. Having crates re-moved could mean extra drayage charges.

In the next chapter, you will see exactly how each of these services operate on the show floor.

5

Setup on the show floor

NOW THAT WE HAVE COVERED GETTING READY FOR THE SHOW BY TAKING care of the paperwork and schedules, it's time for setup on the show floor. In this chapter, you'll learn how to manage setup and save money while doing it. You'll learn:

- *Who's who on the show floor.* You'll find out who is responsible for what services, who you go to when things go wrong, and who to compliment when things go right.

- *Ten simple steps to easy setup.* You'll get an overview of the setup process that will help you plan your own setup.

- *A case study diary.* You'll discover through a custom exhibit setup case study how to solve problems on the show floor.

- *How exhibit maintenance works.* You'll learn how maintenance of your exhibit is handled during the show, including what to do about storage and security.

- *How to dismantle.* You'll learn how to dismantle your exhibit and deal with the aftermath. When the show closes, your work's not quite done. With these tips, even dismantling will go smoothly.

After reading this chapter, you should be well-prepared to go out and manage your setup with confidence. It's easy once you know the rules and the players.

Before you can manage setup, however, you need to know what to wear during setup, or more precisely, what not to wear. Don't show up in a suit or other "corporate" business garb, you'll be marked as someone who doesn't know what he is doing, a "pigeon" ripe for rip-off. The show floor during setup is just another construction site, so dress accordingly. The accepted attire for setup is jeans and a tee-shirt or sweatshirt, or in hot weather, shorts. Work clothes, that's what you want. Wear comfortable shoes, because you'll be walking miles and miles.

As you begin working on setup, be mindful of your valuables—wallet, purse, briefcase—and leave expensive jewelry in the safe at the hotel or at home. There are thousands of stories about the theft of these items on the show floor or coming to, or returning from, it. Exhibit halls are at least as dangerous as the neighborhoods they are in, which are not always the best.

Who's who on the show floor

In order to make your job easier, you must know who the important people are on the show floor—the ones who can get things done for you and the people who can help you. While some of the people are not "on the show floor," you need to know about all of them. Think about this as you read, who does the money flow from and to? Knowing those facts will explain a lot about how you, the exhibitor, are treated by each of them.

Show owner

Who owns the show? A person, corporation or association? The show owner is the final authority—where the chain of command ends. If the show owner is an association, the slant of the show is usually toward the education and enrichment of its members. If the owner is a corporation or an individual, the personal enrichment factor is an important one.

Show promoter

Sometimes, the show owner will hire a group of people to promote the show, which really means sell the space. This firm will often develop slick brochures and sell the exhibit space through direct mail and telemarketing. Often, these groups will also advertise space sales as well. If you notice a particularly hard selling style, chances are that you could be talking to a rep group, who are hired by the show promoter.

Show manager

For you, the exhibitor, this is probably the most important person with whom you deal. He or she will make most of the critical decisions, and these directly or indirectly affect you.

Show managers are likely to decide on the layout of the floor plan, assignment of space, appointment of the official contractors, and resolving exhibitor complaints. A good show manager tries to keep everybody happy. It's not an easy job.

Official contractors

Official contractors are appointed by the show manager and include florist, and photographers, the set up and tear down people, and the cleaners. They are the contractors whose work orders you will find in the exhibitor kit. They have been reviewed, checked for performance, and tested by the show manager. Most experienced show managers have their favorites, who perform well and at fair prices (which might include a fee given back to the show manager or show owner).

Official hotels/travel agents

The same arrangements with official contractors are also made with hotels. In fact, one show owner reportedly will not take his show to certain cities because he can't get fees back from them. Official travel agents work the same way.

Independent contractors

Independent contractors are also called nonofficial contractors by show management and official contractors. These are the service firms hired by exhibitors that are not contractors appointed by show management.

Typically, exhibitors have the right to hire their own contractors to photograph their exhibit, clean it, or put plants in it. Usually, the exhibitors also have the right to hire an installation and dismantle firm to supervise the laborers in the setting up and dismantling of the exhibit. Sometimes, the exhibitor can even hire a private work crew of their own choosing to do the work.

The answers to the question, "Which service can I hire if I so desire?" can be found in your space contract. When you sign it, you agree to many things, and often included among them are references to nonofficial laborers and labor supervisors. All but the strictest show owners will allow you to bring in an outside supervisor, provided he or she has insurance.

Unions

In a right-to-work state, you and your full-time company employees have the right to put up and take down your own exhibit. Those states are: Alabama, Arizona, Arkansas, Florida, Georgia, Idaho, Iowa, Kansas, Louisiana, Mississippi, Nebraska, Nevada, North Carolina, South Carolina, North Dakota, South Dakota, Tennessee, Texas, Utah, Virginia, and Wyoming.

In each facility, the unions have negotiated, often long and hard, for the right to do a certain specific type of work for you. For instance, the riggers earned the right to hang all of the signs.

What might be less clear is who gets to handle the crates the hanging signs come in, the riggers or the carpenters? Each union has a specifically negotiated right of jurisdiction over work done on the show floor. Obviously, over the course of a year, that jurisdiction represents quite a lot of money to the union and its members. As they see it, exhibitors are taking bread off their table when they try to do the work that clearly falls within their union's jurisdiction.

Even in facilities where you have a choice, it is "appreciated" when you use laborers from the union labor pool. The general belief is that things go a lot more smoothly for you if you use union laborers. There is no thinly veiled threat implied here. It's just that your use of union labor shows your support of the unions, and unions like that. All of this might sound confusing to a newcomer but it simply boils down to these few points:

- You can always set up your own exhibit if it can be set up in under 30 minutes and without tools.
- In a right-to-work state, you can set up your own exhibit using company personnel.
- In all other states, you do not have the right to set up your own exhibit unless you can do it in under 30 minutes, without tools.

Read the contract for any deviations to these guidelines. Unions set official break times and quitting and clean-up times. Typically, a union worker is entitled to a break in the morning and in the afternoon in addition to their hour-long lunch break. Often, union workers are entitled to stop work before the official quitting time to clean up and return tools. Check local customs when picking up your labor crew.

In order to save the most money, you'll want to avoid the overtime trap and do as much work as you can on straight time, because it will cost you less. Sometimes, all set up must be done over a weekend, which means overtime. Examine the set up schedule carefully and determine what you need to do to get as much of the exhibit set up completed on straight time as you can.

Ten simple steps to an easy setup

There are 10 easy steps to most exhibit setups, and if you do them in order, there will be fewer problems. For example, an exhibitor might try to unload the crate contents before getting the carpet down. The carpet needs to be down first so that you don't have to move all of the exhibit pieces later to clear a path for the carpet. Most are just plain common sense that can keep setup running smoothly and on time. The first five steps happen before any exhibitry gets put together and the last five takes the exhibit through to completion. Now let's have a closer look at each.

Step 1. Check your space

Upon arrival at the hall, go right to your exhibit space and check that it is exactly the space for which you contracted. Is the show laid out exactly the same as on the last update of the floor plan? Is your booth the proper size? Does it seem to be lined up with other exhibits? Do you see any competitors in nearby booths, and will that cause a problem for you? One exhibitor arrived to find that the hall was completely revised and that their worst competitor was directly across the aisle.

Step 2. Check your services

The next thing to do after checking your space is to stop at the service desk and confirm your service orders. If you have been keeping good records and called two weeks prior to the show to make sure everything is in order, you are now likely to see some faces that were only voices on the phone. If something has gone wrong, check in your site book, which should be with you. Get to the hall early so that you can confirm your service orders long before you expect the freight to arrive. This way you'll be ready for it whenever it comes.

Step 3. Be there when the freight arrives

You need to check with your transportation provider just before the show to find out when you can expect your shipment at the hall. If you are using a van line that has a representative on the floor, he or she will be able to keep you updated.

This step is most important for exhibitors with custom exhibits who will be using large labor crews for setup. They will want to get the best and freshest crew possible for their elaborate setup, and the good workers go early.

The game plan at this point is to estimate the time of arrival of your freight and try to get the crew to arrive at the same time. A crew brought in too early means wasted time and money as they stand around with nothing to do. A crew brought in too late means time wasted, which could mean more work to do on overtime later on. Admittedly, there are occasions when, in order to get the best crew, you claim them early and have them drink some coffee, just to prevent the good ones from going back into the labor pool.

Direct the draymen delivering the crates to set them around the periphery of the exhibit. It's a nice touch if you can get them to set the crates in order. Your crates should be numbered and you should have a crate contents list. That way you know the exact location of every panel and graphic.

Some draymen will complain that you can't put the freight in the aisles because you will be blocking them. What they might want you to do is put your freight in the booth space and then have to pay to move it again in order to set up the exhibit. Stand firm unless you see that the aisles are already full and there really is no other place to put it.

A well-laid out hall governed by a smart show manager will run smoothly in this regard, and there will be enough room for everyone's crates without too much of a problem. Of course, it always looks a mess, but that's part of the charm of setup.

You will not be allowed to put your crates in major cross aisles, because there are the "highways" of main traffic. Don't stand around out there, because you might be run over by a fast moving forklift. Should an accident occur, file any damage claims as soon as possible. If you are shipping lots of freight to shows and have problems with damage, it is a good idea to keep an instant camera on hand to document any damage as soon as you spot it and file damage claims immediately.

Getting satisfaction on damage claims can be one of the most frustrating things you will come up against. The best advice from those who have succeeded is to document what you can, get witnesses, and speak up immediately. If you get to the booth and your shipment is already there and it's damaged, you cannot be certain who did the damage. Was it a drayman or was it the transportation provider? If you are there when it comes off the truck and spot the damage, then you know at which point it was damaged.

Step 4. Get the crew

Again, be at the hall as early as possible to get the freshest crew. If your freight arrives at 2:30 in the afternoon and your setup schedule allows it, wait until the next morning to start. A crew you get at 8:00 AM will be alert to your instructions and be ready to understand your first directions.

Be sure to always sign your crew out and back in. Never, repeat, never depend on a worker signing himself out or in. And check the time cards kept at the contractor's desk daily for accuracy. It's not a bad idea to keep your own records also.

Step 5. Get your crew ready

Introduce yourself to each member of the crew and tell them your name and that you will be supervising the set up. Then take a few moments to review the setup drawings. Keep a copy in your site book just in case those packed in the exhibit get lost.

A photo of the completed exhibit should be attached to each setup graphics in a hall where the electricians union has strict jurisdiction. In Chicago, for example, expect the electrician to insist upon coming back to do that for you, as well as replacing any light bulbs.

Step 9. Details and clean up

About three quarters of the way through a large setup, the exhibit will look like a bomb went off in it and not much progress is taking place. This is the time to start the clean up process. From this point on, clean up should be a main part of the activity.

You can also start to unload literature or giveaways into secure storage areas, putting wastebaskets in place, setting furniture, wiping down graphic panels and doing touch-up cleaning or painting on the exhibit structure. If you start cleanup any earlier than this, whatever you clean up will just get messed up again.

Step 10. Pack up

The last step is to check all of the crates and boxes one last time for anything you need, close them back up, and put an empty sticker on them so they can be sent to storage. The empty sticker needs to have your company name and booth number on it.

When you put the empty sticker on your crates, remove or obscure all old labels. There are many stories about exhibits being shipped to the wrong location because an old label wasn't removed.

Try to store as many boxes and small crates as you can in nooks and crannies of the exhibit so you can start some of the packing-up as soon as the show closes. This way you are able to do something while waiting for the crates to come back from storage.

Here's a tip. Things move into and out of storage on the LIFO system, that is, last in first out. Therefore, hold off as long as possible before putting the empty stickers on your crates.

Well, that's setup and, you now know more about it than two-thirds of all exhibitors. So don't have any reservations about going out on the show floor and giving it a try. If you want the very best in luxury and service to make setup trouble-free, hire a van line that specializes in trade shows and has a supervisor on the floor plus an installation and dismantle firm and their supervisor. This way, you have two supervisors taking care of the difficult parts—transportation, drayage, and labor—and you are left to just manage the process.

A custom exhibit case study

Now that you have the big picture and know about the 10-step method of setup, here's a case study, in diary form, to illustrate how it works on the show floor. This diary is for an exhibitor using a custom exhibit. As you read comes up from the floor within your space, it will need to then go out to all points within your booth. If it comes to you through a line from other places on the show floor, then it will enter your booth through a channel and that will create a big bump under both the aisle carpet and at the spot where it enters your booth.

In all three cases, you need to do a little thinking about where the electrical is coming from and where it needs to go. If the electrician has not made it to your part of the hall by the time you are ready to start laying the carpet, just lay down some cord and then later you can snake up the lines by tying the cord to the lines.

You might want to use a plastic covering over the carpet to protect it during setup. It can be laid right over the carpet with the exhibit structure set up on top of it. Just before show opening, it is stripped away. It pulls off cleanly because of the weight of the exhibitry making a nice straight edge. This is only done for large exhibits or light-colored or expensive carpets.

Step 7. Start setting up

If you have a custom exhibit, you can save time (and that means money) by having all of the crates in order and having a crate contents list. This way, you can tell the workers exactly where they can find the next panel or graphic.

Typically, exhibits are set up by starting at one end and working out to the other for an in-line exhibit and starting in the middle and working out for an island booth. The bulk of the structure is roughly set in place and then when the entire exhibit is assembled, the crew can go back and make any small adjustments to it. The graphics and pedestals are left till later so that the exhibit is lighter in weight, making any fine-tuning easier. Once the structure is placed exactly, all bolts should be checked to make sure the panels match with tight seams. Sometimes when the hall floor is uneven, shims (little wedges of wood) are needed to steady the structure.

Now stand back and check the work. Does everything line up and do all the seams look tight? Walk around and touch all of the panels, testing for sturdiness.

Of course, if you are using a portable exhibit, setup will be greatly simplified. You will still need to have the carpet laid, but if you order it from the official contractor, you will probably find it ready when you arrive. With a ten-foot portable, you will be setting it up yourself. You can do it in under 30 minutes, without tools.

Step 8. Set the graphics

Once the structure is in place, it's time to hang the graphics and connect the electrical by plugging in everything. This step usually goes fast and without many problems. One thing to watch for is plugging in the lights or lightbox drawing. If the crew can see the finished exhibit, it will be easier for them to assemble it. A small crew setting up a simple exhibit will need much less direction than a big crew setting up a large complex exhibit. If supervising a large labor crew is not high on your list of professional skills, hire a supervisor. Supervisors will ensure that your exhibit gets set up as quickly and economically as possible. You can get a supervisor through an independent installation and dismantle firm or from some official contractors who offer "custom services." Supervisors can make your life much easier.

One of the important things you need to do shortly after explaining the setup drawings is go buy everyone coffee. It is the smart thing to do. It shows the crew that you are a decent person and will also tell you what kind of crew you have. Take special note of how long you are gone and how much work has been done while you are away. If they goofed-off, you will need to supervise this particular crew very carefully. If they got down to work, the rest of setup will probably go quickly.

Always treat your crew well, with coffee in the morning and soft drinks in the early afternoon and even a beer just before the end of the day. Doughnuts and chips help, too. If your company has giveaways, like caps, tee-shirts, or key chains, pass these out to the laborers as an incentive. Treating the crew decently makes the work go much faster and that saves you money.

Those are the first five steps that get you ready to start the setup. From here on out, the dust flies.

Step 6. Lay the carpet

All halls, except for those in hotels, have concrete floors, which makes laying carpet fairly easy. You just roll out the padding, if you are using padding, stretch it a bit, then roll out the carpet on top of it, stretch that and tape it down.

If you are in a hotel and are laying carpet over carpet, you won't need padding. No matter how well the carpet is laid, it will stretch when laid over other carpet. The only way to prevent this is to first set down a base of plywood.

If cost savings are your interest and you are in a hotel ballroom that's carpeted, consider not using another carpet on top of it. Just remember that carpeting in these ballrooms is usually of a unique and bright pattern and might clash with your exhibit.

Before you start laying carpet, plan where electrical lines will go. If you are in an in-line booth (a row of 10 × 10-foot exhibits), then electrical services will come from the dead space at the rear of your exhibit. If you are in an island space, the electrical service will either come from overhead, up from the floor within your space, or by a line from elsewhere in the hall. If the line drops from overhead, it should drop into a section of the exhibit structure and feed out under the carpet to all points within the booth. If it it, note the contrast with the set up case study of the portable exhibit in chapter 4.

Thursday: Arrive at show city. The plan is to do as much setup on Friday as possible, which is straight time. Some work will have to be done on Saturday, which is overtime, but with luck, not too much. Hope to take Sunday off.

Friday 7:30 AM: Get to hall and check space. (Step 1: Check you space.) It aligns with the aisles and it resembles the latest floor plan. No competitors are near.

The freight, which was not scheduled to arrive until this morning is already in the booth. (Step 3: Be there when the freight arrives.) Now the laborers will have to spend about 15 or 20 minutes arranging the crates and boxes before they can begin work.

Check the crates for damage and hope that there is none because it will make filing a damage claim impossible. No damage: breathe a sigh of relief. Remind self that this is why we bought insurance.

8:00 AM: Take site book to the labor desk and check about picking up a crew of four. (Step 2: Check your services.) They are very busy, and I find my labor order form before they find theirs. They show no record of payment having been sent. My copies of the check and the return receipt are in the site book. They back down and smile a lot.

Ask for three workers I had last year. (Step 4: Get the crew.) Get two of them and two new ones. Sign them out and we all go back to the pile of crates in the booth.

Explain how crates should be set and where they can find the setup drawings (Step 5: Get your crew ready.) Then take coffee orders and visit the snack bar. Snack bar is close to the service desk so stop and see about electrical. I take the site book everywhere. Our area is the next to be done. On to the snack bar.

Upon returning to the booth, one of the new workers is sitting on the roll of carpet, but the other three have organized the crates in numerical order and are looking at the setup drawings. Make a mental note to keep an eye on the one sitting down.

Pass out the coffee and doughnuts as we review the photos and set-up plans. The older guy comments that he remembers this exhibit from last year. He seems sharp and I bet he does.

Direct the crew to start laying carpet. (Step 6: Lay the carpet.) It is difficult for more than two laborers to lay carpet, so watch to see who pitches in and who takes it easy. The older guy and one of the new guys dig in. The other worker from last year helps by getting things organized.

The one sitting on the carpet from before is standing around watching. I now know that he will be dragging his feet all the way along. When his hour is up, I will comment to the crew that it looks like we only need three workers after all and then sign him back into the labor pool. Then if we do actually need four, I'll go get someone else a little later.

The carpet is down over snakes for the electrical and the three good workers are just starting to set the center structure (Step 7: Start setting up.) Then the electrician shows up. He and I review our electrical needs and he starts. This slows down the workers a little because they have to work around him, but things are moving along.

Right after the mid-morning break, estimate that the electrician will be finished by noon and so go to the service desk to tell them another worker will be needed after lunch. The woman at the desk apologized for the previous mix-up about payment. We chat, and I ask her if she can get me a good worker because I have a hard working crew and don't want to break their momentum with someone who doesn't pull their own weight. She says she'll try.

Noon: Break for lunch.

1:00 PM: Crew is back to work. Go to labor desk to pick up one more laborer. Woman at desk says she has no one for me right now. Check back in an hour.

2:00 PM: Stop at labor desk and pick up a new worker. After getting her started, take orders for soft drinks.

4:00 PM: Setup has been going smoothly. Sign crew back in just at 4:00, which concludes straight time. Tell labor desk will only need two workers for tomorrow, as we are about finished.

Just before going back to hotel, check crates for all graphic panels. (Step 8: Set the graphics.)

Disaster. One is missing. Double check crate contents against the crate contents list in the site book. No doubt, it's missing. Call exhibit house. They will look for it there and call me in half an hour. Tell them to call at the hotel.

I'm tired and agitated. Is anything else missing, because if it is, I need to know about it now. The exhibit house is closed tomorrow. Grab the site book and review the crate contents list. Everything else is here.

5:00 PM: Back to the hotel. The exhibit house has found the missing graphics panel and will send it overnight. It should be at the hall by mid-morning. Because the problem was caused by them, they will pay for the freight.

Saturday 7:30 AM: Back at the hall again. By 8:00, have my crew of two and they have their coffee. Take a minute with them to review our progress and what lies ahead. Tell them about the missing panel. Start where we left off, with the graphics.

Mid-morning: The graphics are almost in place and the product pedestals are next. The exhibit is starting to come together, except for the mess. I start to straighten up. (Step 9: Details and cleanup.)

11:00 AM: Return one laborer and keep the other to help put the finishing touches on the exhibit. The missing graphic panel arrives.

Noon: On the way to the snack bar, I pick up the two imprinters, checking them with my own card. If I wait too long, all of the good ones will be gone.

1:00 PM: Back to work. This is the last hour before returning the laborer. He lifts the literature cases into place, then is returned to the labor pool.

2:00 PM: (Step 10: Pack up.) One last look in all the crates, then fill out and affix the "empty" labels and remove the old shipping labels. Take out the paper towels and wipe down all of the surfaces. Could have had the laborer do it but Saturday is overtime and I am saving money.

4:30 PM: Back to the hotel. Know I've walked 75 miles today.

This exhibitor was well organized. However, that doesn't mean the complete avoidance of problems, just the reduction in the number of them. The freight was already in the booth when she arrived, even though she had received an estimated delivery time the week before. The labor order was paid in advance, but it took them a few minutes to discover that at the desk. Our exhibitor was prepared with all documentation to support her position that it had been paid, which kept her relationship with the official contractor on a positive note.

One of the workers was not the most energetic, and so she diplomatically returned him to the labor pool and later got a replacement, thereby avoiding any confrontation with the worker. The missing graphics panel could have been a disaster, but because she checked her inventory while the exhibit house was still open, it was not.

During the show

Once the show opens, there is a lot less to do. Check the exhibit about once an hour for cleanliness and order. Every evening do a security check and gather up all the leads, put away all the literature and supplies like pens, staplers, etc.

Rip-offs and scams

There are some rip-off artists found almost everywhere, even on show floors. Here are some scams that have come to my attention.

Drayage.   The drayman will bring half of your exhibit to your booth and tell you that's all there is. You say that half is missing. He tells you that he would like to hunt for it but is busy right now, but for a tip ($10, $20, or $50, depending on how expensive your suit looks), he can drop everything and search for it. Then he goes to find your freight—in the next aisle, right where he just left it.

Time tickets.   The official labor contractor keeps records of how many hours the laborers spend working at your exhibit. If you don't sign the workers in and out, you are leaving yourself open for problems. Some workers will be very conscientious about going directly from your booth back to the labor desk. The lazy and dishonest ones take hours to get there. Check the time tickets and always sign your workers in and out.

Jurisdiction.   You always have the right to set up your own exhibit if you can do it in under 30 minutes. If some union member tries to tell you otherwise, get his or her name and see the show manager. Because jurisdictions are loosely held to in some cities and strictly held to in others, it is possible that, at some point, you could be doing work in your exhibit and have a union representative say that you can't do that work. If it seems unusual, then simply ask that person to accompany you to the labor desk so you can better understand the jurisdictions that apply in this hall. Be warned that in some halls the jurisdictions are so strict that you cannot change a light bulb without a union electrician.

Tips and bribes.   It is acceptable to offer a cash tip to a worker who performs outstandingly for you. Some exhibitors like to tip, but the majority never offer cash tips. Instead, they give their labor crew other incentives, like food, beverages, or giveaways. Some halls even post signs discouraging tipping.

Bribes are something else. At a New York hotel, one exhibitor was told that she could not get the electrical service she ordered until she paid the electrician $20. That's extortion. If you are asked for a bribe, take the name of the individual soliciting the bribe and complain vigorously to the show manager.

Early wash-up.   Your crew might tell you that they are entitled to more wash-up time than they should actually get. Just inquire about the standard breaks and wash-up times for the hall when you pick up your labor crew.

Outbound shipments.   The official contractor for freight is entitled to ship all not previously consigned pieces of freight. In other words, if you just leave your freight on the floor with no other freight designation, the official freight contractor will take the responsibility of shipping it.

In some cases, the official freight contractor will get over zealous and "pirate" shipments assigned to other carriers. This causes the exhibitor problems when their freight is missing and does not show up for some weeks. Avoid this by being in close contact with your own carrier. If your freight is pirated, report it to show management so that they can become aware of their unscrupulous contractor.

Dismantle: no big deal

Dismantle needs just a little organization to run smoothly. Typically, it takes about half the time to tear down an exhibit as it did to set it up. The key to a smooth dismantle is getting the same crew you used for setup. This crew knows both the exhibit and how you like to work. Next, check the crate return schedule to estimate when your crates will be out. If your crates were one of the first sent into storage, they will probably be among the last to be returned. While you rest and wait for the crates, think about what you would do differently the next time and any repairs that need to be made. Now is the time to make note of anything that will make your life easier the next time around.

By now, you should feel confident enough about planning and managing setup that you can manage just about any challenge you'll meet. Appendix A contains the most common "What if . . ." situations and how to handle them. Once you read that, you'll be prepared for anything!

6

Leads and follow-up

LEADS ARE THE REASON WHY THE VAST MAJORITY OF EXHIBITORS GO TO shows. Some might actually write orders on the show floor but most take business cards or write leads. If you write orders at shows, then skip the first part of this chapter. Otherwise, read it all. You'll discover three critical concepts that will make the difference between being profitable at shows or just fooling around:

1. What makes a great lead form. You need a lead form that is short and sweet, fits into your hand, and is always ready to use.

2. Follow-up. You need to be quick about follow-up because your competitors will be.

3. Tracking and reporting results. You must find out, in terms of dollars and cents, how the show performed for you. You must evaluate.

Sounds simple, don't they? You would think that most exhibitors use a lead form and follow-up in a reasonable amount of time. Yet most exhibitors, both large and small, miss at least two out of the three critical concepts and a surprising number miss all three.

Leads represent the return on your substantial trade show investment. When the show is over and everything is packed up and shipped off, the only thing you have left for the money you spent is the stack of leads in your hand. When you understand this, you start to care very much about those leads and start to think about what happens to them, so if you want to get serious about shows, then you first have to get serious about leads.

What makes a great lead form

What is a lead form? It's a simple piece of paper that causes many other things to happen. A lead form can be a prompt in the qualifying process. It can indicate a next step to take, like sending literature or making a sales call. It can make life easy or hard for the salesperson doing the follow-up. It can provide research data about your visitor's interests, even preferences. It can provide another name for your mailing list. This one little piece of paper can do all of that . . . if you take time to think about the potential it holds and design it so that it gives you what you need. In this section you will find out:

- How to simplify data collection by tying into the show registration system.
- What makes a good lead form.
- How staffers should use lead forms.

Tapping into the show registration system

Sometimes, you can make lead gathering easier by designing the lead form with an eye to the show registration system and using the information already captured when the visitor's badge was produced. Doing this saves your staffers time because they don't have to duplicate work already done for them by show management. If you attend business shows, be aware that every one of them in America registers their attendees. At these shows, some of the work involved in capturing visitor data might already have been done for you.

The way shows produce badges and register attendees can determine how you can generate leads most efficiently. Smaller shows usually give their registrants paper badges, and those are of no help to you if there is no mechanism by which you can share the data captured on the badge. Larger shows, however, often give attendees credit card-type plastic badges that you can run through an imprinter (which are rented to exhibitors for use in their exhibit), to capture the most basic data: name, company or affiliation, address, and even phone number.

Registration systems are getting more sophisticated, and a few shows now use magnetic strips on the badges encoded with the attendees name and address. At these events, exhibitors rent mag strip readers. Some shows use similar technology to scan bar codes on the badges.

Another method for easy capture of visitor data is found at some shows using paper badges. Each attendee is given a unique number that is prominently displayed on the badge. The exhibitor can make a notation of the badge number and then, at the end of the day or end of the show, request the data from show management.

The advantage to the scanner and badge number systems is their ease of use. The bad news is that exhibit staffers get lazy and tend to record no more data than the limited amount of information on the badge. When they do this they lose the opportunity to get much more in-depth information from the visitor.

If you attend different shows that use a variety of registration systems, then you might need a variety of lead forms that dovetail into each. Some exhibitors have two types of lead forms, one for the credit card-type badge systems and another upon which the visitor data must be written. No matter what the shows registration system, it makes sense to design your lead forms so that you can tap into it. Not all shows are diligent about getting 100 percent accurate registration data, however, so you might want to spot-check the accuracy of the data on the badges by asking your visitors if it is correct. An exhibitor found that at one show, about 30 percent of the badges contained some incorrect data.

What a good lead form isn't

A business card does not make a good lead form. There was a time years ago when it was sufficient to simply take a visitor's business card and jot a few notes on the back. But today, it's a whole different, competitive world out there. You can get a feel for how competitive shows are by comparing the "jot a few notes on the back of the card" method of lead taking to the sophisticated lead forms in use right now.

A good lead form is not the generic lead forms you get from show management. Those are just slightly better than writing on the back of a business card. These generic lead forms are far from the ideal sales tool. Why? Because they do not accommodate the specific information you will uncover in the qualification process. They are not customized or detailed. You will need a customized lead form that helps staffers remember the information to go after—a sort of prompt. If you get nothing else out of this book, get this: you need a custom lead form. Don't worry about cost, because it only takes about $50 or less to do it.

The key to great leads

The physical attributes of a lead form are important. If it is too big, too small, too thin, or doesn't contain the right spaces to fill in, then it will not do the job and staffers will not use it. One poorly designed lead form resulted in no leads taken for the new products because there was no check box for it. The following are three simple steps to designing a lead form that staffers will use:

1. Make it small. A good lead form is small and fits into your open hand. It is about the size of a large credit card form.

2. Put a backing on it. A card stock backing on it will give staffers a surface to write on when holding it in their hand. See Fig. 6-1.

3. Make it multipart. Multipart lead forms can be especially useful. You can send one copy to fulfillment, which will be sending out the literature packages; another to sort the hot leads for immediate follow-up; and the last to keep as a permanent record.

The key to great leads is having a place for all the right information. Figure 6-2 shows an example of a well-designed lead form. Take a moment to look at it and consider all of the information and its relevance to you. Here are some comments about each area on the sample lead form and the decisions you must make about the design of your own lead card:

- *Vital Information.* Included here are show name, name, title, address, and phone number. It is a good idea to use *Company* or *Affiliation* because professionals and government employees do not have a company. A very useful question to include after the space for phone number is, "Best time to call." Some of the information might be on the badge, and if you have tapped into the show registration system, capturing this data will be easy.

- *Business/Industry.* Is this information of interest? If you sell to just one industry, this might not be needed. If you sell to a variety of industries that are not always clear from the company title, however, this cate-

Fig. 6-1. This staffer completes a multipart lead form with a card-stock backing that fits in his hand.

Lead Form

Name _____

Title _____

Affiliation _____

Address _____

City _____ State _____ Zip _____

Phone _____

Best time to call _____

Product Interest:

[ ] Product A   [ ] Product B   [ ] Product C

Application: _____

Current Client?:

[ ] Y Representative _____

[ ] N Now using? _____

Business/industry _____

Time frame

[ ] 0–3 Months   [ ] 3–6 M   [ ] 6–12 M   [ ] 12+ M

Qty/time

_____

Budget: _____

Comments: _____

_____

Decision maker: Y   N   Who _____

Rating   A   B   C   D

Lead taken by

_____

Show _____ Date _____

Fig. 6-2. Sample lead form.

gory might be useful. Try to use check boxes here and wherever you can because they speed up completion of the form.

- *Client.* Is this individual currently a client, and if so, who is his account representative? If not, which competitors are they using?

- *Product interest.* If you have many products, think about using product family check boxes followed by fill in the blanks for the specific product designations.

- *Application.* Use check boxes if you can. This one is important to those exhibitors showing products that can be used by a number of industries in a number of ways.

- *Time frame.* This is very important to ask and to capture on the lead form because it is going to be one of the factors that will help prioritize follow-up.

- *Budget.* This is an interesting entry, because some exhibitors always ask about the budget and others avoid it. True, in some industries it is inappropriate to ask about budget so early, but the vast majority of exhibitors just don't have the nerve to ask it.

- *Quantity/time.* How much of the product would they need and over what period of time?

- *Now using?* How are they meeting their needs right now? A variation of this is to ask if they are a customer and, it not, what are they using at present. This will also tell you if they are using a competitor's product/service.

- *Comments.* This can be one of the most useful spaces on the lead form where other information can be captured, even by your own sales people.

- *Decision maker.* Is this individual the key decision maker and, if not, who is?

- *Rating.* A rating helps prioritize follow-up. There are many ways to rate a lead; one of the most common systems is A = hot, B = warm, C = send literature only. A simpler system is to not call it a rating and offer a choice of one of two follow-up actions: 1) have salesperson call or 2) send literature.

- *Lead taken by.* Knowing who took the lead can be useful when you can't read the writing. By getting staffers to sign the leads, you can track them back to the source.

- *Show name and date.* This can be written or stamped on each lead so you always know the source.

Perhaps you are thinking that this is far too little or too much information. In fact, it is just the right amount. If you require too much more, the visitor gets restless and is uncomfortable about answering so many questions. If you require any less, you don't get all of the information for successful qualifying and follow-up.

Additionally, if there are other things you want to know about the visitors to your exhibit, appropriate questions can be put on the lead form. Just remember that visitors will answer just so many questions and no more. One exhibitor used a full-page questionnaire-style lead form that would only get half completed before the visitors called it "quits." Some of the most important questions were at the end, rendering the leads just about useless. Keep extra research questions to a minimum of three or four, and put your most important questions up front after the critical qualifying data.

Fine-tuning your lead form

Obviously, the design of the lead form will shift slightly depending on how your company sells its products or services. The lead form shown in Fig. 6-2 is appropriate for those exhibitors doing hard product sales. Look now at the next two lead forms shown in Figs. 6-3 and 6-4. These should be used by companies that use applications selling styles and consultative selling styles. Take a moment to compare and contrast all three.

In these lead forms, the selling style determines the structure of information on the form. Note that the fullest one is the one for hard-driven product/commodity selling. It might seem that the other two forms are set up to capture less information, but they are not. It's just that the information on these forms is less structured because the selling style is less structured. Just remember, however, that, although the structure for capturing the data is more free-form, the leads should be just as completely filled out as any other.

In an emergency!

If you ever find yourself at a show without lead forms, just go to the stationery supply store and get 3-by-5-inch index cards. They are large enough to accommodate all qualifying data but small enough to fit into the hand. If no

Lead Form

Name _____

Title _____

Affiliation _____

Address _____

City _____ State _____ Zip _____

Phone _____

Best time to call _____

Interest:

[ ] Product A   [ ] Product B   [ ] Product C

Application: _____

Other equipment: _____

Time frame

[ ] 0–3 Months   [ ] 3–6 M   [ ] 6–12 M   [ ] 12 + M

Comments:

Rating   A   B   C

Lead taken by

_____

Show _____ Date _____

Fig. 6-3. Applications-oriented lead form.

Lead Form

Name _____

Title _____

Affiliation _____

Address _____

City _____ State _____ Zip _____

Phone _____

Best time to call: _____

Interest:

    [ ] Product A
    [ ] Product B
    [ ] Product C

Comments:

FOLLOW-UP: [ ] Send literature   [ ] Sales call

Lead taken by
Show _____ Date _____

Fig. 6-4. Relationship/partnership lead form.

stores are open, try the business office at the hotel or show hall. Index cards are much more useful than standard blank imprinter forms because there is more room to write and a firmer surface.

When to use lead forms

It might seem that taking a lead is the simplest process imaginable. That is almost right, but there is one thing to remember: start using the lead form early. Most staffers wait until the very end of the conversation before jotting down notes. Then they feel pressed for time and leave off data that could be useful. Other cultures, like the Japanese, do not think of this as lead taking but as data collecting and therefore, are highly methodical about accurately recording all of the data. Unfortunately, we Americans rush.

When a staffer starts to use the lead form very early as a place to write notes, he or she is working in a more consultative manner, and that's good.

The staffer might draw attention to their note taking by involving the visitor, and asking, "Do you mind if I make a note of that?" Or the staffer could just say something like, "That's important. I better write it down."

The exhibit staffer might choose not to announce the entry of the lead form into the interaction at all, and simply start taking notes. In any of these situations, the use of the lead form in this manner, early in the interaction, sets a very consultative tone, which adds a positive dimension.

Keep them ready (but not too ready)

Some exhibitors have the staffers put the leads on a small clipboard or in a folder or notepad, which they carry in their hand at all times. In this case, the lead form is ever ready, which at first glance appears to be good. This is a very sophisticated technique, however, that can, if not handled properly, make the staffers look like a bunch of order takers ready to "write up the deal." This style is unattractively aggressive and not appropriate for an exhibit. Visitors are usually intimidated by the experience of entering your selling space so, your objective is to increase, not decrease, their comfort level.

If there is any doubt about how your people will handle the clipboards or notepads, don't use them. Instead just keep the lead form in a pocket or on a nearby counter (see Fig. 6-5) or other part of the exhibit within easy reach.

If your exhibit is larger than a 10- × -10-foot space, you will need to keep the lead forms in multiple locations. The objective is to enter the lead form into the exchange as early as possible, and that will be inconvenient if the staffer has to go very far to find one.

Incomplete lead forms

There is hardly an exhibitor who has not complained that one of their biggest problems is getting the staffers to completely fill out the lead forms. The most common reason for incomplete forms is that most staffers feel rushed, and that means they do not take the time needed to fill out the form. They typically wait until the last minute before the visitor leaves to start writing up a lead. At that point, they are rushed because they can see that the visitor has mentally closed down and is ready to move on. Rather than try to control the situation and slow the visitor, the staffer is controlled by the visitor. All he needs to do is say, "Now this part is important. I must be sure that we have correct information here so that we can better serve you," then take the time to fill out the form completely. Other situations that can lead to incomplete lead forms include:

Staffer attitudes. Occasionally, staffer misconceptions cause problems. They simply do not understand that visitors can be asked qualifying questions and that they should make notes in the presence of the visitor. I

Fig. 6-5. This staffer is using a custom lead stand. It is compact but contains every-thing he needs—blank lead forms, imprinter, pens, and a secure box for completed forms.

did a training session for a highly technical new venture that was just build-ing its sales staff by drawing from their engineering ranks. These engineers were brilliant, but not well-schooled in the most common ground rules of selling. They were appalled at the thought of actually letting the visitor see them write down comments on the lead form. They thought it was too "salesey." After much discussion, they finally saw that if a staffer really cares about solving the visitor's problem or serving a need, he needs to fully docu-ment it on the lead card. If staffers don't care, they won't make any notes. Taking the time to fill out the lead form shows respect for your visitor.

Missing information.   There is missing information and then there is MISSING INFORMATION. Missing time frame information is a bother, but a missing phone number can make a lead unusable. One cause of this com-mon problem is simple sloppiness. Another cause is perceiving that a lead is less qualified and consciously not caring if data is incomplete. For instance, a staffer uncovers some piece of information that indicates that a visitor is less likely to buy, such as the time frame is too long or there is a committee or board that controls the company/association and that this visitor is not the final decision maker. At this point, the staffer loses interest and stops asking qualifying questions—and no more data gets captured. Staffers should be encouraged to complete the entire qualification process and ask all of the pertinent questions before turning in the lead card. There is no telling how much influence a visitor might have over the buying decisions of others in the company, especially in smaller associations and corporations.

The cure for missing data is accountability

Staffers will do better at getting all of the data on the lead form if they know they are accountable for it. You can help ensure that there is accountability for complete lead forms by having staffers initial, sign, or affix a personal code number to their leads.

If incomplete lead forms really plague you, consider an incentive program that rewards staffers for complete leads or have a booth captain check all the leads every half hour. Sometimes, the qualifying question has been asked, but the staffer just forgot to write it down. By the team leader reviewing the leads, you ensure that every last drop of information makes its way to the lead form and into the follow-up process.

Follow-up

A well-designed and professionally executed lead form is worthless if follow-up isn't done properly—or collected properly. An exhibit rental company owner reports that when their rental stands are returned, about 30 percent come back with the leads still in them. Hard to believe, isn't it? Consequently, before you can even begin follow-up, you must first assign someone to collect all of the leads daily and see to it that they get to the next point in the process. Otherwise, you could become part of that 30 percent statistic.

If your lead form has multiple parts, you can send one copy to the fulfillment people who will be sending out the literature packages, another can be used to sort the hot leads for immediate follow-up from the others, and the last copy is for you to keep as a permanent record.

Fast is best

Some exhibitors take pride in getting their literature in the hands of the prospect fast. They will overnight the leads to the fulfillment house or home office and the literature will be sent out by first class mail the next day. The idea is to have a literature package on the prospect's desk when he or she returns from the show.

Other exhibitors feel that this is too quick and that their literature package will just get lost in the stack of mail waiting in the in-basket. These exhibitors plan so that the prospect gets their literature the week following the show, when there is less competition in the in-basket for his or her attention.

Although there are two schools of thought here, the main point is that the literature needs to get into the hands of the prospect quickly, so that when your salespeople make the follow-up phone call, the prospect already has the literature on his or her desk. Also, exhibitors have probably already forgotten you, but a quick look at your literature will quickly jog their memory. Finally, if many of your competitors were at the same show but your literature arrives first, leads are more likely to perceive your company as efficient.

Fulfillment

How and when you use literature with your exhibiting efforts is called your literature strategy. Like many exhibitors, you've probably not given much thought to your literary strategy. Take Sam Helm for instance, he found after a recent show that they were giving out the same brochure at the show, mailing it in the follow-up literature package, and expecting that the salesperson would use it on their first sales call. This is overkill.

Their literary strategy was later revised and they decided to forgo literature in the booth, design a junior version of the piece for follow-up mailing, saving on postage, and leave the punch of the main literature piece for the salesperson's use. This is a good literature strategy.

You'll have to decide exactly what goes into your fulfillment package sent after the show. Some exhibitors personalize cover letters with each prospect's name, address, etc. Others save on this expense, which can be substantial, and use a preprinted cover letter. Some exhibitors assemble each literature kit individually, based on the interests of each visitor. Others send the same literature package to all of the prospects. If you are using a service to perform this function, it will cost more to customize each package rather than using the same literature package for all lead fulfillment.

Exhibitors with a small volume of leads usually take care of the fulfillment themselves, while those sending out 200 or more leads per month usually go to a fulfillment house.

Should you use telemarketing?

You might want to use telemarketing follow-up if it is important to verify the qualifying information prior to sending salespeople out in the field. Also, if you are providing leads to distributors and your leads are competing with other manufacturer's leads for their attention telemarketing might be the edge you need. Another example of the wise use of telemarketing is if you have a small, overworked sales force that has precious little time to spend on lead follow-up and needs to devote their energies to only the very best of them.

You might be wondering why you would need to phone the same prospects just seen face to face at the show. Telemarketers who follow up show leads find that 20 to 30 percent of the information on lead forms change between the time of the show and the time they are followed up. Therefore, if you must have the very best data, then you should use telemarketing follow-up.

Clerical details that matter

There are two logistical details that you will need to think about:

1. How are the leads going to be sorted by sales territory?
2. How are they going to be prioritized so that the best ones are taken care of first?

Sorting by sales territory. If you have a sales staff and if you are taking fewer than 200 leads per month, they will probably be sorted by hand and the person doing the sorting will need a list of sales territories. If you are processing the leads through a fulfillment or inquiry processing house, one of the first things they will ask about is a zip code breakdown of your sales territories. From then on, the sorting will be done by a computer. The trick in both instances is to be sure they always have the latest list.

Prioritizing. If you have designed the lead form with a rating system, like A, B, etc., then it is very simple to prioritize them.

Some exhibitors use a two-vector rating system based on the urgency and volume or size of budget. Those prospects with the greatest dollar potential and the shortest time frame get the most immediate attention.

Although both of these logistical points sound simple, they become impossible if the lead form is poorly designed and doesn't include the right information.

Tracking and reporting results

Tracking and reporting the results of your exhibit efforts are the final steps of exhibiting that are most often overlooked. After all, the show is over, the leads have been sent out, and exhibitors are anxious to get on with other things. It takes relatively little effort to analyze the aftermath, and the resulting information is vital to determining whether your exhibiting efforts were a success or whether you need to change your focus. The results should give you some indication as to which shows are best for giving you the type of leads that you need. Are some shows better for decision makers or a particular product? Analyzing the leads will give you the answers you seek.

Lead tracking

A good place to start analyzing your results is with your leads. Lead tracking involves following a prospect until there is a final disposition; either a prospect purchased or they didn't. Often, it also involves identifying the dollar volume of business generated by the lead. This is called a sales conversion study, which results in a return on investment analysis:

$$\begin{array}{ccc} \text{Return} & : & \text{Investment} \\ \text{(from sales conversion studies)} & & \text{(all direct costs)} \end{array}$$

The simple return on investment ratio serves as a guide to evaluating your trade show efforts and gives you a benchmark in which you can compare individual show results. You can easily track the "Investment" side of the ratio, but the tricky part is measuring the "Return" side. The closer the sale is to the time of the show, the easier your task in calculating the return. If there are months or even years between the show and the sale, try having your sales force estimate the return based on two factors: 1) percent probability that the sale will happen and 2) dollar volume of the sale. Then factor those out and use that number to estimate the return. A good return on investment is $6 to $1, or for every $1 you spend on the show, you get $6 back.

Although it is easier for some exhibitors than others, sales conversion analysis and return on investment calculations are one of the most valuable ways to evaluate your results.

Simple lead analysis

Lead analysis means that you, usually with the aid of a computer, wring out of the raw data on the lead forms all of the information that you can. Some of the types of information you should be able to analyze include:

- Audience interest in products. Can be by show, month, year, or geographically.
- Audience interest in product applications. Can be by show, month, year, or geographically.
- Analysis of the range of time frames. Can help to forecast business cycles.
- Percent of leads that were "Hot." Helps evaluate show audiences.
- Percent of leads with other ratings, including "Literature only." Helps evaluate show audiences.
- Geographical breakdown. Can uncover new geographic markets.
- Business or industry category breakdown. Can uncover new market segments.
- Analysis of the range of budget. (Can help forecast business cycles or compare shows.)

Mailing list dynamite

If you have automated the lead fulfillment and dispersal process, then you have at your fingertips one of the best mailing lists you could ever hope to find. From this data base, you can get lists of individuals with specific product interest or applications; or you can get a list for just one geographical area. All of which can be used to do preshow mailings or other promotional mailings.

Using a leads fulfillment house

Handling leads can be a problem. They need to be taken care of quickly, and for most organizations, it's difficult to allocate the resources and dedicate the time to analyzing leads. It is also an intermittent job. One month there might be 2,000, the next month none. That's why many exhibitors seek out handling services or fulfillment houses. Should you decide to use an outside service, however, there are a number of things to keep in mind.

The first is deciding what you want the service to do—personalized letters, standard and individualized literature packages (they pick from your literature inventoried at their location), distribution of leads to the field, lead tracking, telemarketing, and a wide variety of reports—then compare services. All of these services can be had for a price, but just be sure to decide what you really need before talking to them. Listen to their description of the standard service, including the costs; then compare their standard service to what you think you need. If you need more than what they customarily offer, they either might not be able to accommodate you or it will be too expensive to modify their system to suit your needs.

Check a number of references thoroughly, and inspect the facility before you decide. If they look sloppy, they probably are. Don't chance all of your hard lead work with a substandard operation.

You should expect a start-up fee ranging from $1,500 to $3,000. This pays for the initial set up of their system for your use. You will also need to provide a list of your sales territories and alert them every time it changes and keep them stocked with literature.

All of this might sound like too much trouble, but when the choices are either handling the leads yourself within your own company or sending them to a lead fulfillment house, it can pay to send them out. By giving them to a fulfillment house, you are assured that the leads are properly taken care of. The extra benefit is that you will automatically get the lead source analyses reports you need. That alone is worth the price.

In the final analysis, leads are the reason most exhibitors make the investment of time and money in any show. Doesn't it make sense to spend just a little more time and money to design a usable lead form, follow them up fast, and analyze the results?

Part II
The strategies

7

Planning for success

GOOD TRADE SHOW PLANNING IS EASY. BAD PLANNING IS LONG AND HARD. IF you think planning and setting objectives take too much time, get ready to do some hard hitting, easy, and streamlined planning designed to make your exhibiting very successful. By following the instructions in this chapter, you'll take careful aim at your competitors through a well-thought-out plan that uses just the right amount of your precious resources, and you'll find yourself way ahead of the pack.

Doing your planning work

You should apply about 50 percent of the brain power you spend on exhibiting to planning because it is the step that drives everything else you do. Exhibitors who are wildly successful all have one thing in common: they have done their planning work. Take the Brown brothers for example.

The Brown brothers took over their father's small chemical company when he retired. The company was a very small also-ran in their sector of the industry, but the brothers were optimistic about the potential for growth because the market wasn't overcrowded. They felt that attending some trade shows could generate sales quickly and help the business to grow, and that's exactly what happened.

At shows, they drew attention to the new product, a high value import from Switzerland, by having their exhibit staffers work the aisle offering passers-by Swiss chocolates. They opened conversations by saying, "We're giving out Swiss chocolates to celebrate our new product imported from Switzerland. Would you like one?" As the attendee took the candy, the staffer quickly asked, "Would you like to register for the Swiss watches we are giving away each hour?" As the staffers signed up prospects for the drawing, they also inquired about the visitor's work environment and any need for their new product.

Because the featured new product was a quality item, quality drove everything they did at the show. The exhibit was given a special look, the chocolates were the very best, the staffers sported boutonnieres on the lapels of their very best business attire. The approach was so successful that they used it at all of the shows they went to that year. The brothers are now enjoying their success and listening to more than one overture to buy the company and make them instant multi-millionaires. Planning pays.

This plan worked in two ways. First, their market started taking notice of the quality image. Second, leads taken at the show jumped from just under 200 per show to well over 2,000 at each and every show they attended. The leads were well-qualified and generated sales beyond their original projections.

Perhaps you would like to try to similarly take advantage of trade show opportunities. But how to start? In this chapter, you'll learn a three-step effective planning method that cuts through the nonessentials so that you can get a plan quickly in place—the same plan the two Brown brothers used.

1. *Identify the strategic elements*. Be your own consultant and ask yourself basic soul-searching questions about the reason your business exists. Here you will be setting both image, objectives, and sales goals.

2. *Develop tactics to reach a strategic objective*. If you intend to capture market share, you'll need to beat out the competition. In this step, you'll develop your own tactics that will do just that.

3. *Design a creative plan*. To mobilize your audience and bring them closer to your objective, you must design a creative plan, perhaps enlisting the aid of an ad agency.

Identifying the strategic elements

In this section, you will do a brainstorming exercise of sorts. It's easy and you *must* start with it. This is not an option. Most people who do this exercise fail to fill in all of the information on the first pass, but do your best, will you? You might even feel a bit self-conscious asking yourself about the details of your company history, but go with it. If you are going to be at all effective when setting objectives and goals, this information has to be down

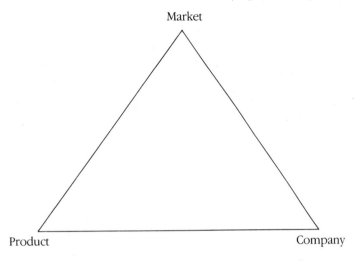

Fig. 7-1. The objectives-setting exercise triangle.

on paper. The exercise is best done with a partner, as it makes it easier and more interesting. Just don't start telling each other what you want to hear. Be brutally honest and watch out for corporate puffery.

The three corners on the triangle shown in Fig. 7-1 represent the market, the company, and the product. Trade shows are where they all come together, and you need to see their interrelation on paper. Get the biggest sheet of paper you can find, like a flip chart pad, plot out the triangle, and label its three corners.

If you are familiar with mind mapping or brainstorming, you'll have some fun here and be way ahead of the game. If not, just relax, don't worry about doing it the "right" way because there is no right way, and enjoy this brainstorming technique.

Now that you have the triangle laid out, let's get to work. Think about the relationship that is created by the two elements on the right side of the triangle: the market and the company. Ask yourself what is important here: what is key in the relationship of your company to the market. (Be sure to separate the company from the products. We are interested in the company right now, and we'll get to the products later.) Is it the long or short history of the company, the personality of the founder, the economic conditions of the marketplace, the sales structure by which you reach that market? What is important? Quick, when I say the name of your company, what does the market bring to mind? Do you have any research on this or are you just using opinion? Write each of these points along the right side of the triangle as you think of them. Be sure to focus on today's conditions, not what they ideally should be. There will be time for that later.

To get a better idea of how this should go, see the example shown in

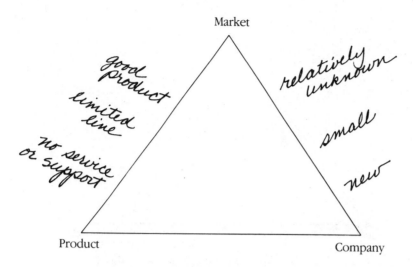

Fig. 7-2. Sample objectives-setting exercise triangle.

Fig. 7-2. In this fictitious example, the company sells mailing systems that include such things as postage meters, scales, and small business packaging centers containing all the supplies needed for shipping, such as boxes, filler, and tape.

Now go to the other side of the triangle and define the relationship between the product(s) and the market. (When we say product here we also mean service, as today, most services are packaged and promoted the same way as products.) Who buys it, why, and when? Who influences them? How do they use it, and what are all of the applications for it? What competes with it directly and indirectly? What is the position in the market for the competitors in contrast to your product's position? Pricing? Delivery? Service and support? And so on. Again, when I say the name of your product(s), what does the market bring to mind? Write these down on the left side of the triangle. Remember, deal with today's situation, not the world as you would like it to be.

Now, on to the last side of the triangle, the relationship of the company to the product(s), what is important to this dynamic? Product mix, margins, availability, enhancements and new releases? Identify all of the existing factors at work within the company as they pertain to the product that might have a significant affect on the strategic or tactical plan you craft. There are usually plenty of important issues that can fit on this line but you only need be concerned with those that will affect this particular planning process.

When you have done this much, you have done most of the real work. You need to do one more thing, however, before you go on. Go back over what you have on the diagram so far and investigate it for hype. Every company has its own mythology that everyone lives and breathes. Ask: Is this really the way the market sees us? If your work is to be good enough to beat

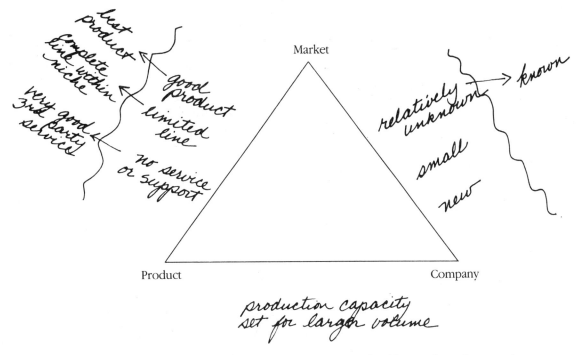

Fig. 7-3. Sample of a completed objectives-setting exercise for The Mailing Systems Company.

the competition, you have to go back over it and take out the hype. Be hard-hearted and totally objective. This is where that second person can be of help.

This represents what exists today, but what about tomorrow? Now, get another color pen, pencil, or marker and enhance this brainstorming map by adding notations on how these relationships should be in the future. Is one of your products a low-priced workhorse and no one knows about it? Did the company have some hard times when the new product failed at an alarming rate but everything is fine now? These are the elements of your image that must change and will be addressed in your tactical plan. See Fig. 7-3 for an example of our mailing systems company.

That's all there is to it! You should have uncovered all of the important pieces in the puzzle without spending too much time on the small issues. Better take one last look to be certain you didn't miss anything, then you are ready to go on to the second step.

Developing tactics to reach a strategic objective

There is a big difference between objectives and goals. Objectives have to do with image. Goals are sales oriented. You desperately need both. The following is an example of an objective we might set for our mailing systems company: we want to be known for quality; a total mailing systems for small businesses.

Be careful not to make your image objectives too self-serving. Lots of image objectives mention leadership. There is an emphasis problem in a statement like, "We want to be the leader in small business mailing systems." The emphasis is self-serving and focuses on what's nice for the company, while ignoring the needs of the consumer. Leadership is great for the company, but quality is what turns on the customer. Remember, your market couldn't care less about your need to be a leader. If you serve your customers well, they'll make you the leader, it will not happen just because you make it your objective. In crafting your own objectives, keep your attention on the market's needs and wants, not those of your company.

Goals concern themselves with sales. Which products do you want to sell and how many do you want to sell? A marketing communications goal often concentrates on leads that can turn into sales. (Except when the communications medium is structured to get sales and book orders at the show, then the sales goal and the marketing communications goal are the same.) A standard marketing communications goal states how many leads, of what type, and which media, and the number of sales generated by those leads. Here is a statement of a very specific marketing communications goal that supports a sales goal.

"50 sales of total mailing systems (priced from $10,000 to $15,000), resulting from 5,000 leads, assuming a conversion rate of 1 percent. The leads will be generated as follows: 1,000 leads from trade shows, 2,000 leads from advertising, 1,000 from public relations, and 1,000 from direct mail."

To make this easier, try to get two different color highlighters. With the first, highlight all of the important points on the triangle that contribute to the image objective. Using the other one, highlight all of the sales goals information. This simple exercise should be a big help as you try to set the image objectives and sales goals.

Most image objective and sales goals are usually workable for a year, so keep that time frame in mind. Next year, revise them.

Often, if a company thinks about setting sales goals and image objectives at all, it simply states what it wants as a goal without realistically referencing where they are at present. After deciding on your objectives and goals, do a "quality check." Remember, the important part of the process at this point is focusing on what the audience wants, not what the company wants. Look very hard at the triangle, which represents a true picture of the product/company/market situation. Are your objectives and goals based on reality, not your wishes for your company to be big and important? If you have market-based goals and objectives, you are well on the way to success.

Strategies for getting and keeping the tactical advantage

Actually developing the strategies for getting and keeping the tactical advantage is both the tough part and the fun part. In this section, you'll learn about some of the tactical moves you can make on the competition. It is the time for putting on the gloves, getting ugly with the competition and, just for a moment, setting aside the needs and wants of the market. In the tactical development stage, the market concern is secondary to outmaneuvering the other guys. That's really what tactics are all about—the competition. Setting objectives and goals ensures that the fruits of the battle will be yours and that you will not return from the show empty-handed, as so many exhibitors do.

Research shows that most exhibitors say that they set the following objectives:

Image building/generate awareness	64%
New product introduction/evaluation	59%
Specific number of leads/new contacts	48%

Research also finds that exhibitors say that they measure effectiveness by these standards:

Count number of leads	78%
Track leads to sales	55%
Feedback from sales department	32%

Now, let's compare the objectives they set side-by-side with the way they measure their effectiveness:

Objectives	Measurement
Image building	Number of leads
Product introduction	Leads to sales
Number of leads	Feedback from sales

(Source: Trade Show Bureau)

As you can see, they don't match up. If exhibitors are going to shows thinking that they are there to accomplish one set of criteria but later evaluate their efforts by another set of criteria, then surely they cannot be happy with the experience. Setting the right goals and objectives is a necessary first step before laying out your tactics.

Some have likened tactics to warfare and others have used chess as an analogy. Both are good examples. If you have six competitors, it possibly feels like you are keeping six chess games going at once. But what you need right now is a list of "obstacles." You are at one end of this path and your image objectives and sales goals are at the other, which is where you want to be. But blocking your path are obstacles, such as the competition. If you are to take the most direct route, you need to identify as many of the obstacles as you can. If you can identify and anticipate them, then you are on the way to overcoming them and reaching your goals and objectives. Start by listing all of the obstacles you can see in the way of reaching those objectives and goals. You will probably end up with statements like, "Competitor A will probably introduce a new product this spring, perhaps at the show," or "Competitor B has the leadership position in the market and takes twice as much space as we do."

Your methods for getting around the obstacles to reach the objectives and goals are the tactics. Now that you have identified obstacles, it is time to select key tactics that will advance you toward your objectives and goals. This is the exciting stuff, where your brain power goes up against that of the competition.

At this point, I cannot tell you exactly what to do because no two company/market/product situations are the same. But what we will do is review six tactical situations, how they work at trade shows, and give an example of each. Then you can decide on the tactics that are right for you. Table 7-1 shows an overview. Now, let's take a look at six common tactical situations.

Table 7-1.
Marketing Tactics

Tactic	Selecting shows and space	Promotion	Exhibit design	Sales style
ON THE ATTACK				
Challenge the leader	stay close to competition	a key element	flashy	hard
Attack their weakness	stay close to competition	a key element	supports promotion	hard
ON THE DEFENSE				
Stay defensive	avoid competition	low key, but powerful	conservative, but modern	dignified
Block a move	take lots of space	can make a difference	stay leading edge	rehearse answers to tough questions
ON THE PROWL				
Make a new market	look for new shows	needed	communicate basics well	
Terrene too troublesome	look for new shows	needed	communicate basics well	

Tactic 1: fireworks

In this situation, you are trying to storm the hill (the market) and knock off the big guys. They are powerfully entrenched, and you know you won't beat them at their own game, so you use fireworks to shift some of the attention of the market from them to you. Your goal is to decrease their share by whatever means you can.

Here's an example. After quite a long time in the business, a computer company was still fighting for name recognition. Tired of getting no respect, they went to a large computer show and raffled off a car every day. They instantly became the talk of the show and the latest "hot" company in the market.

Fireworks work well to create immediate impact, as this one did. However, the problem with a firefight is its flash-in-the-pan nature. Two months later, the computer company was right back where they started because they didn't use the fireworks to start a long-lasting blaze. This computer company should have tied in the car giveaway to its advertising and public relations campaigns and hit hard with a direct sales blitz immediately following the show, which they did not.

One of the first years that Apple Computer exhibited at a major computer industry show they were barely known. They had the guts to dig deep in their pockets and give away thousands of complimentary tickets to Disneyland. It was the buzz of the show, just like the car giveaway. Afterward, they were very aggressive about meeting with the press to make sure their activities at the show were well covered. Apple, unlike the other company, kept up the assault with mailings and ads.

If you are not winning at the game as the leaders have organized it, cause bedlam on the field and make a new game, just as these exhibitors have done. Warning: you will probably be building lots of traffic, and if you do, be sure to discuss it with show management. For the most part, unless you are consistently making far too much noise, smoke, or a nasty smell, show management loves the excitement of imaginative exhibitor promotions because they make the show something to talk about. Consider the fire laws, however, and don't block the aisles too badly with the crowds you draw. Every once in a while is acceptable, but nonstop will bring the authorities down on your neck and might even cause them to shut your exhibit down.

Tactic 2: hit hard at their weakness

In Tactic 2 you go for the leader's soft underbelly. Hit them low, and hit them hard. To use this one successfully, you must target the attack carefully. If you don't hit the mark squarely, it could boomerang.

One of the best tactics is to invite a direct comparison between your product and that of the competition. Prime Computer did that when they sent out a preshow mailer inviting a direct comparison of their CAD/CAM equipment with all competing products. It was outstanding primarily because it provided a checklist of product feature/benefits to better highlight Prime's superiority. They even included a map of the show floor to help prospects find the competition.

Another exhibitor, DCA, used a live presentation to directly attack the competition's weakness. This high technology company used a fifties theme and actors sang the laments of Big Blue, an Elvislike character, the big man on campus who broke their hearts when he got too big and important for them. Big Blue is, of course, IBM, and this little competitor touched on the fears of many small business owners, namely that they are too small to deal with a company the size of IBM. When using this strategy, pick the soft spot and hit hard.

Tactic 3: leaders need to play defensive

The theory behind playing defensive is that leaders must be ready to defend an attack, and one of the best positions to defend from is as high up on the mountain as possible. For this reason, leaders work to distance themselves from any followers.

Being the leader can be rough, especially if you are the leader in a heavily populated market or niche because everyone is out gunning for you. The usual strategy is to get the biggest lead you can and run as fast as you can to keep it. If this describes you, keep the head start by using trade shows to capture the imagination of the marketplace, all at once. Apple Computer has always used very imaginative exhibit designs, including the year that they announced the MacIntosh computer. The product was revolutionary and the booth design matched. It was the first post-modern exhibit I had ever seen, and it stopped me dead in my tracks.

The very essence of trade shows is well suited for the type of big splash that tends to keep leaders ahead and create new leaders in emerging industries. Shows give all exhibitors almost instant access to industry opinion makers and the press—all at once—so that a powerful message or promotion will be delivered to an entire market within three days. Because shows are visual, an exhibitor can change an image overnight. Exhibitors who cleverly use all of the tools at hand can make a statement with copy as well as exhibit design—if they are gutsy.

Often, the leader's exhibit will spotlight research or their historical commitment to the market as part of their leadership platform. These can be as boring as a stone or as exciting as tomorrow, depending on the imagination of the ad agency or other creative people, such as the exhibit designer.

One of my favorite leadership strategies comes from IBM. I watched them work this tactic from afar in the late seventies and early eighties, long before they became a client of mine. They have been known to offer a trade show "sneak preview" of a product that is coming down the road in a year or two to their key clients. This obviously does a couple of things for IBM. First, it keeps them deeply entrenched in the leadership position as innovators (where they want to be), because it indicates that they have important products coming just around the corner. Next, it makes their clients feel special when they are asked to sign confidentiality agreements about new products being previewed to them. It tells these clients that they are important and in the "in crowd." Third, it gets the client committed to that yet-to-be-released product. And if the word leaks out, no harm done, because the entire market knows IBM has something coming out in that product position and any company thinking about a product release with a similar position will have Big Blue to contend with. It's a very smart tactic and drives the competition crazy.

The essential aspect of using trade shows to maintain leadership is quality. No matter what you do as a leader, it must reek of quality. As a leader, you cannot get away with giving out cheap trinkets and trash (the common derogatory term for low-quality advertising specialties.) Your promotions must be imaginative and inspired, that is if you want to guard your leadership spot.

Tactic 4: block a move on your territory

Obviously, it makes sense to block a move on your territory by a competitor if you want it to remain your territory. Here is a simple but elegant example. A small military technologies company exhibited at the industry show in Washington, D.C. The market for their product grew steadily. After the election year, it looked even more promising because of a new administration that supported increased military funding. Consequently, a very large company moved in on their market and the show.

Every year the show opened with a lavish cocktail party for the military brass and their spouses. It was customary for exhibitors to have small giveaways like flowers or key chains available at the reception.

The exhibits manager for the smaller company called the show manager and explained that he didn't want to duplicate any giveaway someone else might be offering, so would the show manager please tell him what others were doing? Yes, the show manager would. The big company, he found out, was giving roses to the spouses. Long stemmed, he inquired? Yes.

At the reception, the generals and spouses would get a long-stemmed red rose at the big company's booth. Then at the little leader's booth, someone would offer them a short, elegant crystal bud vase. The natural thing to do was to put the rose in the vase. But when a too long rose stuck out of the lovely, short crystal vase, the rose looked silly. The staffers had scissors on hand to cut the rose down to size.

What a metaphor! The perishable, too long, too obvious red rose, versus the sturdy, enduring quality of the crystal vase. Not to mention cutting the rose down to size. Now that's blocking a move!

Tactic 5: go after fresh territory

If the market you are in is overcrowded, go after another market, or even a niche. The example used in the opening pages of the introduction to this book is really an example of just that. The key to the doll manufacturer's success was in their approach to the giftware market. They did not go after stores that already carried dolls, instead they pursued stores that did not presently carry dolls but were willing to agree to carry their doll alone. Typically, these stores had thought of dolls as toys, but were made to see the potential of dolls as a gift speciality. If there was only one type of doll for customers to choose from, it became a unique gift item.

Attacking fresh territory usually requires some educating. Either your prospects have never heard of your product or never thought of your product/service as the preferred solution, or had just never thought of that situation as a problem before. In any case, trying to educate an entire market to the fact that they now have a problem and you have a solution can be a difficult task. Difficult, but worthwhile.

Pharmaceutical companies all suffer the long lead times required to develop products under FDA guidelines. Many pharmaceutical exhibitors, prior to getting FDA approval, will take a large island exhibit at key medical conventions to educate physicians about certain problems they face. The problems are stated in a very educational and informative manner and the exhibits often have a museum quality. This education makes the physicians aware and softens the market for a new product release.

Tactic 6: take the business no one else wants

Another way to address the needs of a market is to go after the business no one else wants. Sometimes, no one else wants it because it is too troublesome, or sometimes it is just hidden. Take someone else's problem and turn it into your solution. Here's an example.

Luxury car owners often don't have the time to take care of their cars the way they would like but they will spend considerable dollars on "automobile detailing," or custom car cleaning. One West Coast retailer had five shops in the Los Angeles area and wanted to go national through franchising. The plan was to reach prospective franchisers at trade shows on franchising. He was very excited because, based on test marketing at two shows in the Midwest, he felt that he could sell about 100 franchises in the upcoming six months. He was reaching out in a very big way through trade shows to solve the specific, troublesome problems of marketing in a niche.

Each of the these six methods used tactics that rely on promotion, space

Fig. 7-4. This health care exhibitor features a problem, not a product, prior to getting FDA approval for the product.

selection practices, exhibit design, and the selling strategy in very specific ways. Take another look at Table 7-1, which lays it out at a glance.

Tactics one and two are similar in that both are aggressive, flashy, and sometimes, even risky. Tactics three and four are similar to each other in that the leader is fortifying its position and acts very much like a leader in doing so. Tactics five and six help an organization break new ground. If you have not done so already, identify the appropriate strategy for your company or product. Then use this as a jumping off point to complete your tactical planning and start thinking about your Creative Plan.

Implementing a creative plan

At this point, you have done some streamlined brainstorming, set your image objectives and sales goals, and thought about possible tactical maneuvers that will help you take your leadership spot in the market, which in turn will aid you in reaching those sales goals. Next comes the "creative" planning part, turning all of this work into a very real exhibit program with all of the pieces, such as the exhibit design and show promotions. Here is where the smart folks turn it over to the professionals, such as the ad agency, the exhibit designer, or the exhibit house's promotional arm.

No matter how small your budget might be, never ever try to do this part yourself unless you are a very talented in-house creative professional with training. Some sales or marketing people think that when the planning is finished, the hard part is done. Or perhaps they might suddenly feel the need to dabble with an exhibit design because the creative part looks either easy or fun. If this describes you, then don't do it, because it will look like you did it. Get a professional who knows what they are doing.

What is lacking in many of the portable exhibits seen today is good design. Many times, the structure is quite excellent, but the graphics are awful. When asked about the design process behind the finished product, the owners of the awful exhibits invariably confess that they did it themselves. This is unfortunate because in most cases, there was fine design help available through the exhibit supplier, and at no additional charge.

Why then didn't these exhibitors take advantage of the free creative services? There are two answers. First, some of these exhibitors stated strongly that they knew exactly what they wanted and told the exhibit sales representative as much. The sales rep just gave them what they asked for. Second, if the exhibit buyer appeared to know that they wanted, the salesperson might finish up the design without the input of the design staff, thus keeping design costs down and thereby leaving the staff free for other projects. Moral of the story: if your exhibit includes a design service, be open-minded enough to take advantage of it. And if it doesn't include design, be wise enough to seek out the counsel of a professional. Go outside for professional creative help and when you do, be ready to share your tactical plan with them.

Write it down

I own a small company, so I know how busy a business owner is. You're lucky to have the time to think a plan through, never mind writing it all down. We must always remember that others must implement these plans of ours, however. Do them a big favor and take about 15 minutes to jot down the highlights of your plan. Those who will be struggling to understand exactly what you had in mind will appreciate even a few bulleted points scratched on the back of a used envelope. If you expect them to do a credible job, give them credible input.

8

Exhibit design

THIS CHAPTER COVERS A TOPIC THAT IS MORE INNATELY INTERESTING—
exhibit design. Almost everyone feels that they know a thing or two about
this subject, or at least they know what they like, which is true to a degree.
Although not all of us have the talent to design exhibits, we do have a sense
about whether we are drawn to an exhibit or not and whether it is communicating something to us or not.

When we're on the show floor, it's easy to spot good design if we see it.
It reaches out to us, it excites us. It's also just as easy for us to spot bad
design when we come upon it. However, back at the shop or office, if we're
very close to the design process, our vision gets clouded, making it difficult
to evaluate the work at hand—and that can be dangerous.

While walking down a side aisle, at a major health care conference, my
progress was halted by possibly the ugliest exhibit ever designed. This one
was a study in everything you shouldn't do. The exhibit structure was a per-
fectly fine portable with a dark blue velcro backdrop. On the backdrop was
copy panel after copy panel jammed full of text, some with very small intri-
cate illustrations, scattered everywhere. As if that wasn't enough to confuse
attendees, it looked as though every piece of literature or photograph of
their product was also added to the exhibit. The only thing missing was a
clear indication of who they were or what they did.

In this chapter, we will examine the way exhibits communicate and how
to evaluate whether each element of the exhibit supports that communica-

tion. Someone once described an exhibit that didn't communicate as just another pretty edifice, and we don't want that to describe your exhibit. There are also some general observations about how design works, which will help you organize your thinking and communication, as well as some recommendations on finding a good exhibit designer and fabricator.

Planning and design

Your exhibit works in many complex ways to underscore your image. One of the most important things to keep in mind throughout the design process is that everything you do should be done with the visitor in mind. Understand that the impression you call "your image" is created in the visitor's mind almost instantly, regardless of how much planning and strategizing you've done. Conversely, no matter how little time you put into crafting your company's image or how haphazardly and casually you approach the business of using design to create an image, you are competing against companies that have, in some cases, spent millions of dollars using the best talent in the world. This is your competition for the attendee's mind.

If you have done your planning work, you should feel ready to meet the competition squarely and give direction to those working on translating your planning into an effective exhibit design. Let's look at that tactical chart in Table 8-1, concentrating on the column headed Design Recommendations.

_____ **Table 8-1.** _____

Planning Tactical And Design

Tactic	Design Recommendation
#1 Challenge the leader	When lighting fireworks and going up against the leader, be flashy. Try leading-edge design, trendy colors, the latest in materials and techniques. Your exhibit must be flashier than the competitors.
#2 Attack the leader's weakness	Use a strong promotion or theme exhibit that goes right after the leader's weak spot. Tie in the exhibit design to the theme.
#3 Leader stays defensive	Use the same strategy that has brought you to a leadership position, usually a bit conservative, but not always. Try design that is a bit more modern, but not trendy, unless that's what got you where you are.
#4 Block a move on your territory	This is a very delicate spot. Often, you don't know you need to block until it's too late. If you do know in advance and can find out how the competitor will attack, this will help plan your defense. If you anticipate a move but don't know the exact nature of the move, anticipate all possibilities and be as ready as possible.
#5 Fresh terrain	In this spot, concentrate on doing the basics well, like communicating who you are and what you do. You are starting from the ground up.

As you can see, various design tactics are needed for each of the planning tactics listed. Find your own situation on the chart and consider the recommended design approach. Is it right for you?

Types of space and exhibit

Once you have decided on your image, it's time to focus on how much space you need (which you should have figured out if you have been through chapter 5) and what type. Obviously, your space parameters are a primary guideline in designing the exhibit. There are three types of space: in-line, peninsula, and island. Each as its advantages and disadvantages as described in Table 8-2.

If you have been through chapter 5, you understand the variables involving traffic flow throughout the exhibit hall. Now consider how traffic will flow past and into your exhibit. If you are in an in-line space, traffic might come from just one direction. Or is there something happening in the hall that would indicate that it might come from both directions? If you are on a corner, will it come from three or four directions? These same questions must be asked if you are in a peninsula or island space as well. Also, are you near food halls, seminar rooms, or lounges?

Traffic pattern analysis is important because main messages and attention-getting design devices should be oriented toward the bulk of the traffic. If traffic is flowing in two or more directions, the devices should be repeated.

How exhibits communicate

The business of how exhibits communicate is a complex one. It involves colors, and words, light, sound, marketing messages, and giveaways—all in three dimensions and real time. It is an experience that has impact beyond the scope of print advertising, one that is memorable for months, even years.

Table 8-2.
Space Evaluation

	Advantages	Disadvantages
In-line	Economical Scattered throughout the hall	Weaker impact Sides and back of hall
Peninsula	Can use in-line exhibit Greater depth means more visitors Three aisles means good exposure	Watch show regulations on line of sight
Island	Usually in good traffic areas Exposure on four sides	Expensive

Here's an example that was at the same show as the ugly exhibit mentioned earlier in the chapter. To this day, most people who saw this exhibit remember the name of the company even though many have never used their product.

The demonstration that left such an impact was for defibrillator paddles used to zap an unbeating heart. The defibrillator certainly couldn't be demonstrated on a person, so they were using a chicken from the supermarket. The chicken, a nice size one, was set up on the corner of two aisles, and when a small group of three or more people would walk by, a sales staffer would zap the chicken and its little body would flick all around. It unfailingly caught the attention of the passers-by, who knew what they were looking at. A small crowd would gather and staffers would swing into action. Then later, when things got slow again, they'd put the chicken back to work and another crowd would form.

While this example might be a bit bizarre, as you consider it, remember that impact like this goes well beyond the scope of print advertising. It is impact that's three-dimensional, real-time, live. It is impact that the visitor can participate in with you, where he or she can use all of their senses. To visitors in the chicken booth, the color of the carpet, the chicken, the reaction of the crowd that gathered, are all inseparable. While we, as exhibitors, might be looking at single elements when we discuss design, our visitors are experiencing a whole.

This whole is often referred to as the gestalt, or the experiencing of the whole as an impression. For example, when you walk into a room, you have an instant impression about it. This gestalt is formed not from the individual pieces in the room, but from the relationships of the pieces working together. The same is true in your exhibit; all of the elements are working together. Consequently, you need to review each element of your exhibit and consider the effect it will have on the rest of the environment. This is where your common sense will guide you.

Mindset of visitors

Before you can understand the effects of design on visitors, it is helpful to look at what visitors are thinking and feeling before they actually visit your exhibit. Here are the things we can say about the attendee mindset:

- Most attendees want to be at the show. They personally have made the decision to go. No one told them to go. They have a positive attitude and an open mind that you can take advantage of.

- They are away from the office and are removed from office problems. Often, this distance makes it easier to see the problems for what they are and to evaluate possible solutions. Educational sessions enhance this evaluation of problems. Because problems are more easily seen, so are your solutions.

- They are away from daily pressures and are more relaxed. They are better able to socialize. Because the daily clutter of life at the office and home is removed, they can pause to reflect. They are open to your message.

- They are not in their office or your office. They are, strictly speaking, more neutral territory.

Attracting the visitor

Before we get deeper into what attracts visitors to your exhibit, let's stop and review two common analogies that people think about exhibit design and how it works. It has often been said that it works like three-dimensional advertising. This analogy is weak because it leaves out the most important fourth dimension—time. The chicken exhibit would not have been so effective if the visitor had only seen a photo of the demonstration. What made it memorable was the action going on there.

Another analogy often drawn is that a trade show exhibit works like a billboard in that both must stop people within five to seven seconds. This analogy is better because it concentrates on the need for good stopping power before the opportunity is lost. It still falls short, however, because the billboard stops its work after seven seconds. In an exhibit, the first seven seconds are just the start.

These two metaphors, the three-dimensional advertisement and the billboard, are not perfect because they ignore three design elements that work to attract visitors—color, sound, and light.

Attracting with light

In recent years, light has become increasingly more important as a tool to attracting attention, especially for the larger exhibitors. While some techniques can only be used in large spaces, others will work in small spaces as well. Lighting is a strong element in the design mix. It can create a mood, provide ambiance or drama, or be an integral tool of an exhibit. Some halls are bright, others dark. Most are a dreadful mix of light areas and dark spots. About the only thing you can count on is not having light when you need it and getting too much just when you don't want it.

The first year a certain computer manufacturer demonstrated their LCD portable computer monitor at a show, they had a mini seminar set up in one area of the booth. The plan was that every 20 minutes there was to be another "class" who got a tutorial on the use of the new portable. What they got was a lot of trouble seeing the screen because of improper lighting. This is a good example of when lighting could have been used as a tool to an exhibit.

There are literally hundreds of horror stories about ruined plans due to hall lighting. If the effect of your exhibit depends on a certain lighting, be sure it will work with the lighting available in the hall or arrange your own.

For larger spaces, light can be used to create ambiance. The next time you are at a show, look up at the ceiling for lights turned off over an exhibit. Notice the special lighting in that exhibit. You will probably find extensive theatrical lighting that creates a dramatic effect and sets a mood. The small exhibitor can use lighting to show off products to their best advantage and for signage as well. Fiber optic signs and backlit transparencies are just two of the ways you can add drama to a small exhibit space with light. (See Fig. 8-1.)

Attracting with sounds

Sound also attracts attention. Sound could mean amplified presentations (whether individual or for a group), music to set a mood or as an accompaniment to a presentation, or "canned" presentations, like a slide show, video, or film presentation. Sound can be either a positive or negative element. A positive example would be noise emitting from a demonstration of

Fig. 8-1. The use of light can be seen in this exhibit. The backlit center photo transparency creates a strong, graphic presence while the header lighting reflects off of the copy panels. Skyline Displays, Inc.

your product. Be careful not to disturb neighbors. It is a good idea to chat with them before the show to let them know you will be using sound extensively. Let them know that, if your product demo drives them crazy, they should come talk to you (before complaining to show management.) At a mining show, an equipment demonstration was so loud that it vibrated throughout the hall and was later ordered to be shut down, so keep sound at an acceptable level.

At one industry show, we were across the aisle from a short video presentation that ran continuously. By the end of the show, we knew all of the words and could hum the theme song. At the start of the show, the company owner came over to visit us and said that when we couldn't stand the recording any more, we should let them know and they'd shut it down. Just knowing that we could make it go away was relief enough and we never did ask them to turn it off.

Sound can be a positive element and set just the right mood. One high tech exhibit used subdued lighting and softly played baroque music throughout the show. It created a relaxed, upbeat atmosphere that was a nice change of pace in the show.

Sound can also become sound "clutter," sound that adds nothing to the gestalt. One exhibit featured a chamber music quartet to set the mood in their exhibit. Unfortunately, the show audience was young and the mood of the show was more indicative of rock and roll. Attendees would just stand at the edge of the booth and stare in with a puzzled look on their faces, not entering the space. The quartet had a front spot in the exhibit, but there was no obvious reason for them to be there—no promotional tie in, no theme, no advertising that featured or referenced classical music. One visitor asked a staffer why the quartet was there, and he didn't know either. (Someone should have told him why before the show started.)

Sometimes, sound can set the right mood. Another exhibit at a very creative high tech event featured a classical pianist in the exhibit. Again, there was no tie in with a theme or promotion. In this case, as the pianist began, he kept it very soft, but as he got going, the music got louder and louder until none of the staffers could work within 20 feet of him—a real problem since the booth was only 20 x 30 feet.

Attracting with color

Color can be a powerful agent that attracts attention when placed up high with bright lights, or comforting with calm, soothing tones in the main work areas of the exhibit. A modern, trendy color scheme can send one message instantly to the passer-by and conservative shades can send another message entirely (see Fig. 8-2). Later in this chapter, we will explore all of the ways in which color can be used in addition to attracting attention.

Fig. 8-2. This exhibit attracts attention to its corporate identity with a color band in the header. Skyline Displays, Inc.

As you evaluate your exhibit's color scheme, consider the following questions and issues regarding the uses of color when it works to attract the visitor's attention.

1. Does the color palate reflect the image stated in the plan? If your design position is flashy, the color palate should be flashy.

2. Does the use of color in various sections of the exhibit indicate that sections function? Is the part of the display that needs to work to attract attention brightest? Is the work area neutral? Are signage and graphics bright, dark, or in some way both attention-getting or contrast with the rest of the exhibit making it easy to be seen and read?

Attracting with unique designs

Design can attract attention too. The first exhibit for my company was an award winner. People brought their friends over to touch the rough, sand-like finish that was highly tactile. The exhibit, featured in industry publications, truly became a key element in the launch of our young company and new image (See Fig. 8-3).

Crowds attract even more people

People attract attention and create an image in an instant. In fact, few elements have more power to attract attendees than a booth full of people. If

Fig. 8-3. An unusual design attracts attention and creates an image instantly.

they look like they are having fun, all the better. That is why exhibitors have hired magicians for as long as anyone can remember.

At a particularly dull, highly technical show, one exhibit had a very technical presentation in the center of their booth. As the show opened, a few visitors strolled in, and slowly more and more came to see what was going on. The show opened at 10:00 AM and by just before 11:00, a substantial crowd had built that remained all day long. It reached what can be called "critical mass." In other words, there were enough people already in the exhibit so that it looked interesting to others. It attracted other attendees just because there were so many people.

At another industry show, two magicians in two different booths provided quite a case study for comparing ways to attract and keep crowds. One magician stood on the floor with no microphone and drew a crowd of about eight to ten attendees. In another booth two aisles over, another magician used a platform and a microphone to draw a crowd of about 60 people. If your purpose is to draw a crowd and you want to use people to attract people, give yourself the best chance and don't scrimp on details like a sound system and a stage.

Informing attendees

After your exhibit grabs visitors' attention, the real work begins. You must inform them about who you are and what you do. Have you ever looked at an exhibit and been puzzled by who they were? If so, you are well aware of the need to communicate the basic messages. Here is what your exhibit needs to tell attendees when they first set eyes on you:

1. Who you are.
2. What you do.
3. How you can help them.

That the visitor needs to know who you are is obvious. Is your exhibit doing its part to tell them? Is your logo up high? Can it be seen over the heads of visitors to the booth? How large is it and from how far away can it be seen? Do its colors or the colors surrounding it help bring the eye directly to it?

Not only does the visitor need to know who you are, but he or she needs to know exactly what you do. Many exhibitors will place their logos in a visible position and forget to tell the attendee what they do. If the company name tells all, then so much the better. If not, then you must spell it out. If you need to spell it out, then the easiest thing to do is develop a tag line that can always be used with the logo.

Here's an example of the use of logos, corporate names, product names, and tag lines. There is a small health care company whose corporate name was lesser known than the product names. When they exhibited, they always featured the product names. In the final analysis, this was an unfortunate decision. Eventually, one or two of these products fell by the wayside and the company struggled for visibility. Consequently, the company name is just as important, maybe more so, as the product name. Always put the company name in the top, most visible position.

How you can help the visitor is also an important message. It should be found either in close proximity to the company name and tag line or, if it refers to a product advantage, on a highly visible spot near the product display.

The what-we-do statement is an important one. It should come from your deep understanding of how your product offerings fit into the market.

How should you place these items on the display? The answer is easy.

Consider how people will be moving in and around the exhibit and their line of sight. Will the attendees be able to see your message?

If you are using a theme in the exhibit, it is important to position it so that it too will have strong initial impact. The attendees should be able to see it clearly as they approach your exhibit. Themes usually support a product strategy and it is not necessary for the theme message to have such impact that it would compete with the corporate message.

Supporting messages

Now that we have looked at ways to attract attendees to the exhibit and important informing types of messages, we can move on to supporting messages. There are a variety of supporting devices—signage, graphics, product displays, sales aids, and audio visuals:

- *Signage.* Signage should be of a size and height to be easily seen. The colors should enhance the readability. For example, yellow type on an orange background is not easy to read. Whereas, yellow type on a blue ground, or better still, blue type on a yellow ground, is easiest to read.

- *Graphics.* Any words, illustrations, photos, cutaway drawing, etc. that are purely functional are commonly called *graphics*. Graphics is a term that can be used to refer to *signage* as well. Graphics are meant to be seen at close proximity and their main task is to inform. (See Fig. 8-4.) They also create a special design opportunity. Good graphics should look like they are part of the overall scheme of the design but not at the sacrifice of their functionality.

- *Product Displays.* Product displays can be the most exciting thing in the exhibit (see Fig. 8-5), but far too often they are the most boring aspect of it. Remember, the exciting aspect of being at a trade show is the live immediacy of it. Don't just set your product on a display stand, bring it to life. Here are some examples that should spark your thinking. The next section contains information on which products to show and how much room to give them.

~When the *product is small* the challenge is visibility. One way to do this is to use video so that many people can see it at once. A manufacturer's demo of a quality check could barely be seen by one person, even though at least 50 had gathered for the demonstration. Video was the perfect solution. Can't afford video? Try photo blow-ups of the critical stages of the demo.

~When the product is *too big* to be brought in to a hall, another problem is created. At the mining show, a beautiful scale model with operating parts was fascinating to watch as it demonstrated the product in action. The exhibitor had thoughtfully provided tall stools for visitors to sit on so they could really take time to enjoy it.

~When the product is *too dangerous* to be demonstrated in the exhibit,

Fig. 8-4. Staffers explain the product features/benefits illustrated on this colorful graphics panel.

film or video is the perfect solution. Caterpillar brought the excitement of the work done with their equipment all over the world to a film shown in a theatre in their exhibit. Be careful though. Some exhibitors get into problems when the equipment used to demonstrate their product is more interesting to visitors than the product it is there to demonstrate. Here's an example. A software manufacturer at a publishing show used portable computers to demonstrate their new product. Inquiries about the portable computer outnumbered those about the software by three to one. This response caused them to re-think their approach, and the next year, the equipment was put in a private demo area away from the main traffic. The demo area was then used to make presentations to visitors who had a real interest in the software, not the equipment used to demonstrate it.

~Should it be a "live" or *working demonstration or a static display* of the products? That decision might be made for you if it is against show regulations to display your product in action because it is too noisy or dangerous. If you can show it in action, by all means, do. If you have a number of products that can be demonstrated, can you tie them together in some way? Can you show how they can solve problems in the visitor's work environment? Live and in action is the best way to demonstrate product.

Fig. 8-5. These product displays use large photo transparencies and are accompanied by text panels.

- *Sales Aids.* Sales aids includes anything that helps the sales process and does not fit into any of the previous categories. Sales aids might include audio visuals, erasable boards, a photo portfolio, a tabletop sales presentation, even literature designed to support the one-on-one sales situation.

  Encourage staffers to bring their own sales tools to shows. Taking their own tabletop presentation, set of charts, article reprints and the like, makes them feel more comfortable because they are working with familiar materials.

  One exhibitor's booth had a conference area with a small table and chairs. When the exhibit was updated, the staffers were polled to find out what they wanted in the way of sales tools, and the best suggestion was to use a white board as the top of the conference table. This was ideal because when the staffers conferenced, they needed to sketch out a schematic indicating the customers' situation. Before the white board tabletop was installed, the staffers always had to hunt down pads of paper, which were never large enough.

- *Audio/visuals.* Audio/visuals can augment the sales process as well. An example is a slide or video presentation showing the products or capabilities that are not easily displayed in the exhibit.

Today, there is much misuse of A/V in exhibits. Far too often, exhibitors are tempted to use their 20-minute corporate video to attract attention and they find instead that it plays to an empty aisle. Length of the video is an important factor when considering audio/visual material for use at trade shows to attract attention. If you are thinking about A/V in this way, select a short one- to two-minute segment, structured like a commercial.

A longer A/V program is best used as sales support. For example, the staffer might bring a prospect with a specific question about company capabilities over to the corporate presentation to let them sit with it and absorb it. Longer programs require seating and should be in a relatively quiet location.

- *Activity Centers.* Activity centers are high-density traffic areas with a specific function, such as an information stand, a theater, or a formal demonstration. Anticipate the need for them early in the design process because they can greatly impact the traffic flow and overall balance of the exhibit design. Next, consider three of the most common activity centers: lead or information stands, presentation areas, and conference areas.

  ~*Information stands* should be located conveniently on or near the aisle. In very large exhibits, it makes sense to centrally locate a main information area and then place one or two others in main traffic areas. (See Fig. 8-6.)

  ~*Storage.* This is an activity area designed for your staffers alone. A

Fig. 8-6. This information stand is a high activity area.

storage area will be needed to keep literature, purses, briefcases, and supplies. These can be stored under a display table but be aware of security risks; a locked cabinet is much better. Many staffers have put a purse under the table at the back of the booth only to have it stolen.

~*The lead stand* needs to provide ample room to write and make notes, plus a place to lock up completed lead forms. Don't leave completed lead forms on the top of the counter, as they can easily disappear.

~*Presentations* can be a powerful way to bring visitors to your exhibit. If you are planning on one, remember that they need special elements, like a stage, proper sound system, lighting, and seating.

~*Conference areas*, or private demonstration areas, are another functional element that must be built into, not added on to, an exhibit design. Conferencing usually demands private or semiprivate areas, which calls for walls or half-high walls of some sort. If you are thinking about using a conference area, remember that conferencing areas use up a lot of very expensive booth space, and your need must be great before they can be cost justified. In a small, in-line exhibit, the conference area should be no more than a bench at one end of the exhibit. Consider other options carefully before including a conference area.

Deciding which products to display

If you are having trouble figuring out which products to take to the show or how much space to allocate to each of them, the following guidelines can help organize your thinking.

1. Feature new products. Place them towards the front edge of the exhibit, or in any other high visibility spot. If you think they could really capture the imagination of the market, devote plenty of room to them.

2. Feature hot products. As above, give them any high visibility spot in a high traffic area. Call attention to them with signage, color, sound, and lighting. Try a live presentation to add extra punch.

3. If you have both a new product that has a lot of promise and a hot product that has captured the market's imagination, be sure to give ample space to both. Unless they work together or are more important when they do work together, show them separately at opposite ends of the booth so as to allow each its own thunder. In this situation, look carefully at your space requirements to make certain you do not take too little space to accommodate your entire target market for both products.

4. If you have a slightly more mature product, show it but don't feature it. If it is the only product you have, think about featuring a popular application of it or a hot or interesting new use.

5. If you have a very mature product, look hard for a new application to feature, because visitors come to see what's new and they find that old products are boring. In an exhibit with new, hot, or less mature products, feature those, in that order, over the very mature product.

How design elements work in exhibits

How does design work in exhibits? So far, we have touched on the more functional aspects of design, like how the exhibit can work to attract visitors' attention. Now we will review the major design components, like color, patterns, and shapes. The objective here is to get a working vocabulary, an effective way of speaking about design. This will help you feel confident when talking to your exhibit designer and those who design promotional programs for your show participation.

It is necessary to be comfortable speaking the language of design because it is your responsibility to communicate the thrust of your plan, its image objectives, and sales goals to the design team. It is not their responsibility to drag it out of you. Remember, their design efforts will only be as good as your input. It is through your eyes that they will see your market and products. It is because of your direction that they will succeed or fail in their mission to design a workable exhibit for you.

There are many design elements: tone, shade, color, texture, highlighting, patterns, color palettes, translucency or opacity, shape, continuity, and on and on. We will focus on the most important three—color, pattern, and shape–and how they work in the exhibit.

Color

Color is the easiest element for most exhibitors to work with. Everyone coordinates their own clothes, and the principles of good design and color theory apply to exhibits as well. A bright scarf or tie draws attention to the face in the same way that bright colors in the exhibit might be used to draw attention to a header. Bright colors are attention-getting while dull ones are easier to live with, and dark colors are more somber, setting a serious note.

But how specifically do colors work in an exhibit? How is that different from the way they work elsewhere? Let's reflect on the three previously stated functions of design elements—to attract, to inform, and to support—to see how color works in these three ways.

Color can certainly attract. If a color is bright or if two colors are pleasantly juxtaposed, then the effect can attract one attendee's eye and draw her or him in.

Colors can also be used to underscore an informing element. Signage should pop out at you, and color can help it do that. Product displays that use a color scheme that ties into the overall color scheme of the rest of the exhibit will give the exhibit continuity. If possible, sales aids and promotions should be of the same color scheme as used in the exhibit.

Color also plays a supporting role in the total design. Supporting colors should be neutrals. It is much easier and more inviting to walk into a beige exhibit than a red one. Research has shown that a completely red environment makes us uncomfortable, Certainly, it will attract the attendee's attention, but they will not want to spend much time there because a red environment is too intense.

Any dark colors are too oppressive to be used as a main color throughout the exhibit. Darks and brights are better used as relief from neutrals that are used throughout.

So let's recap what has been covered about color:

- Neutrals are good for the main body of the exhibit.
- Brights and darks are best used in the informing and attracting elements.
- There should be continuity throughout the color scheme for the exhibit.

A question that comes up often concerns the use of the corporate color. "If our corporate color is blue should we have a blue exhibit." Think for a moment. How would you feel walking into an exhibit that was all blue? An all blue exhibit will dilute the punch of the corporate color.

Corporate colors are chosen in the hopes of making a statement. For that reason, they usually work best as accent colors, to help various areas attract and inform. In the previous example, the corporate blue logo and tag line should be on a neutral background, making them more visible. Other accent colors can be used to draw the eye towards it. For example, an orange texture, line, or shape could be used as a device to draw the eye to the logo. In this way, blue becomes special and more powerful.

Pattern

Another major exhibit design element is formed by repeating shapes, like the repeated pattern created by thin stripes of yellow on a grey background. Texture is one type of pattern. The textures of your exhibit carpet against the texture of the backdrop can also make a "design statement." Rough textures form a distinct pattern that is visually interesting and draws the eye to it. A smooth surface will reflect the light and can be less interesting if it is a dull smooth surface or more interesting if it is a polished smooth surface, especially when abutting a textured surface. A nubby wall with polished brass trim will have plenty of visual interest.

Shapes

Shapes such as round or straight edges are also a design element found in exhibits. Straight edges lead the eye quickly along a path and round shapes lead the eye more slowly. Straight edges forming a point can also stop the eye or create a focal point. Curved shapes tend to be inviting, softer, approachable. Straight edges, or angles, tend to be exciting and add lots of visual interest and "visual tension," while curved edges add "visual comfort."

Purchasing a new exhibit

Finding a good exhibit supplier, designer and/or producer, or builder, and purchasing a new exhibit, is like finding a good accountant or ad agency. Everyone has heard stories of malpractice in all professions, which you want to avoid while getting the best work for the investment you make. That's why shopping around rather than going with the source that happens to send a salesperson to see you is the better way to buy an exhibit. The following is a five-step system for finding and working with a supplier to build your new exhibit.

Step 1: what type of exhibit?

The first step is to decide what type of exhibit you want and need. Let's take a look at the two most common, the portable and the custom exhibit.

Portable exhibits are very popular. They are used by large companies to test shows and by small companies as their primary exhibit. They are within every budget. Today, the graphics are spectacular, providing a big impact for a relatively small investment. And they can be stored in the broom closet.

A portable exhibit can typically be set up in under a half hour by one person and is light enough to "carry." Portables vary tremendously so use this checklist for evaluating portable exhibits.

1. How large is a 10-x-10-foot backdrop when it is in the case? What else is in the case? (Lights, literature stand, etc.) What is not included in the case? Can it be shipped UPS? Can you fit it into the car you drive or rent?

2. How much does it weigh when it is in the case? What is the case made of? Is it durable? Does it have handles? Wheels? A separate cart?

3. How long would it take you to set it up if you had only seen it set up once? What setup instructions are provided? A sheet, a booklet, or a video tape? What if you get out on the show floor and can't figure it out, who do you call? What if it breaks during setup, who do you call?

4. Are there any tools required?

5. Does it meet Chicago's strict fire retardant regulations, which is the industry standard?

6. Who will design it? What are their credentials? How long will it take from concept to delivery? What are the steps the supplier typically takes? What involvement do they expect of you? What does the price quote include? Graphics?

7. What are the typical complaints from customers who aren't quite happy? Ask for three references who purchased displays within the last six months.

8. Is this distributor financially sound?

As you can see from the checklist, the issues concerning the purchase of a portable are portability (its weight, packaging), ease of set-up, dealer support (repairs, service, design, reputation).

Custom exhibits are another story. These exhibits have unlimited potential to be unique and spectacular. Because they are custom designed and built especially for you, they can truly express the strategy behind your plan.

In years past, if you wanted a custom exhibit, you looked for an exhibit house that would both design and build the exhibit. Typically, the cost of the design was included with the total price of the exhibit. Some exhibit houses put forth that the design is "free," when they actually included that expense with the total price.

Now you have another option, the independent exhibit designer. These designers specialize in exhibits and offer just design or both design and construction of the exhibit. Those exhibitors who purchase these services separately go that route because it gives them greater control over their design and construction investment.

Independent exhibit designers are relatively new. It was not a very realistic choice for exhibitors until a few years ago because most exhibit houses refused to bid on a design if they couldn't have the whole project. Exhibit houses felt they were at a disadvantage when working with a design that was not of their own making because they could not vouch for the integrity of a design that did not originate with them. What would happen later, they would say, if there was a problem with the exhibit, either during construction or afterward? What if the exhibit collapsed on the show floor causing injury? Who would be blamed?

To the designers, the situation looked as though the exhibit houses were trying to keep the designers out of the construction business, thus keeping all of the business for themselves. If the houses stuck together and wouldn't bid on design, then they could lock out the designers. Additionally, if the exhibit house both designed and built it, then no other exhibit house could bid on it, thereby making it impossible for an exhibitor to get an accurate competitive bid.

Then too, if the house wanted to fool around with the materials and swap one type of a material for the other when building a design from a loose sketch, they could. Few materials are specified on a sketch. When the exhibit house keeps the design work, they have more control over the process.

If you want maximum value for your money, you need the control, and therefore, buying the design separately might be worth the extra effort of dealing with two vendors. Today, many exhibit houses will gladly bid on a design from any legitimate source.

Step 2: locating a supplier

Now you need to locate potential suppliers. If you are in a main metropolitan area, begin by picking up the yellow pages. Beyond that, check a directory published by Exhibitor Publications. It lists all of the portable exhibit systems and the major custom exhibit houses and independent exhibit designers.

One of the best ways to find a good supplier is to simply walk shows and ask exhibitors who built their display. Talk to them about cost, reliability, and service. It won't take you long to come up with a list of reputable firms. The following is a checklist of criteria for judging and evaluating a custom exhibit house:

1. *Size*. How many locations do they have? Where? Who many designers on staff at the location nearest you? How many account executives do they have? What is the size of the warehouse? The shop?

2. *Logistical Services*. Do they have services in all of the locations? What are the services they offer? Design? Will you have direct contact with the designer? Transportation? Who is their traffic manager? Does this person specialize in traffic? Installation? Supervision of installation? Will they do it themselves or use an outside service? Who will go on-site at the first installation after the exhibit is built? For a larger exhibit, it should be a foreman.

3. *What marketing services* are available? Remember, the more of these they have, the more you pay for the overhead. Do they offer planning, show selection, research, promotions, staffer training, evaluation, lead processing, and tracking? In each of these instances, be sure to ask specifically who will do this work. Rather than the account executive it should be done by a specialist that concentrates on marketing services.

4. *References*. Ask for five or six and review them thoroughly. Try to get a feel for creativity, responsiveness, and ethics.

Step 3: spec bid or sole source

Once you have located a list of potential suppliers and had an initial conversation with them, you need to decide how to proceed. You can request a speculative design and bid or go sole source.

Speculative bidding. Traditionally, exhibitors go to three or, in some cases, as many as six, different exhibit suppliers and ask them to come up with a design on speculation (at no charge). Most exhibit houses will ask the exhibitor how many competitors they are up against. If the number is too many, they might withdraw from the competition. In the case of six bidders, any given house will feel that they have a one in six chance at getting the job, and the odds are not favorable. If you use speculative bidding and ask for designs from six different exhibit houses, one or more could drop out, and you might be losing the best. If there are just three competitors, the field is smaller and the situation will seem manageable to all of the competitors.

Even with just three suppliers in the speculative bidding process, you are not guaranteed their best work. The account executives will evaluate the situation, taking stock of the competition, and then give the front office their recommendations on how much effort should go into your design project. If yours is a potentially big account, you will get lots of attention from each competitor. If, on the other hand, you are a small company with a small exhibit and this constitutes your entire exhibit building needs for a while, the amount of effort put into your design will depend on how busy their shop is at the moment and how badly they need the work. This is one reason a smaller exhibitor might want to go with a smaller exhibit house where their business is a larger proportion of the overall volume of work. A smaller exhibit might also want to consider local firms because they have a local reputation to protect.

Sole Source. Another way to work with an exhibit house is to interview them like you would an ad agency or accountant and pick the supplier you think you will be the most comfortable with. This is commonly called going sole source. Your decision will be based on their reputation and the work that they have done for others. In this situation, the exhibit house knows that they have the account and can devote all of their energies to solving your problems, not worrying about the competition.

The exhibit houses love it when you do go sole source because avoiding spec design keeps down their sales cost. If you do go sole source, let them know that you know that you have saved them some sales costs and that you expect to see that resource put back into the design effort and trimmed from the overall costs. You win, they win.

If you don't need many of the capabilities offered by the supplier, then realize that they are included in the overhead which drives up the costs of your exhibit. Even if the exhibit house says that they charge clients separately for these services and that it does not affect the overhead, be assured that when exhibitors get together and compare value for the money, the full-service houses are the most expensive. If you are going to use these services, then go with a full-service house, because they will take care of all of your needs professionally, saving you valuable time and money. If you need them, great. If not, avoid them.

Step 4: negotiations

Now let's talk about negotiations. Before you pick up the phone to call an exhibit house, set a budget. When an account executive asks you what your budget is, give him or her a figure about 15 to 20 percent lower than what you have set. Most exhibitors report that it just doesn't work to simply tell the account exec that the budget is set at just so much and that they aren't going to play games, so neither should the account exec by coming with an exhibit over the set budget.

The bid always comes back just over budget. The story from the account exec is always the same: "Well, I wanted to show you this design solution even though it is over your budget because it's really too good not to show. I thought you had a right to know."

The owner of an exhibit house had this to say about getting good value for the money when buying an exhibit. Most people don't fully understand that an exhibit is a custom structure. It is a prototype and there is risk involved. Every time a house estimates on a design, they put their estimating expertise on the line, because that particular structure has never been built before. An exhibit is not a commodity. Therefore, when someone wants to negotiate price, the purchaser is negotiating for something that is not fixed because the exhibit is not yet built. If the purchaser negotiated 10 percent off the price, he not only gets 10 percent off the price, he gets 10 percent off the quality of the exhibit.

One client who just loved to negotiate really got into high gear when it was time to talk price. Just when we had agreed on price and we sent the client the contract, the guy called to say that the price was too high and that we would have to come down $10,000 or it was no deal.

"I thought about it and told him no problem. Then we cut $10,000 of quality out of the exhibit. So the tough negotiator got less exhibit than he thought he did."

If tough negotiating won't work, what will? There are two things that you can do to cut costs. First, plan way ahead and ask the exhibit house about slow times when they would be willing to build the exhibit at a reduced rate. This keeps the shop busy, workers employed, and helps them with cash flow at a difficult time. The other thing is to ask the exhibit house how they would recommend trimming costs in places where the quality wouldn't be affected.

With a custom exhibit house, expect to get an original design. It sounds like a given, something that one should assume about custom design, but don't. Two of our clients exhibiting in different markets had very, very similar exhibits and, except for color, they were almost identical. Both used the same exhibit house and thought that they had paid for an original design.

On another occasion, while visiting an exhibit house, an exhibitor touched a full graphics model of an exhibit being built in the shop and one company's logo fell off to reveal the logo of another company. He later saw both company's exhibits and they were identical.

True, it's unethical. But it's not just the exhibit houses who act unethical at times. Exhibitors too can act unethical by taking an exhibit design done on spec by one design house to another to build. This is unethical and illegal, and the exhibit house that designed the structure could sue you and the exhibit house that built it.

Step 5: the design process

Expect your exhibit supplier to take the following six steps in the production of a custom exhibit. The time frames here are the most comfortable for your supplier, although we all know that they are willing to do each step in less time. If the work is completed on very short notice, expect some rush charges.

1. *Input meeting.* Bring to the meeting your tactical plan, image objectives, sales goals, product literature, show prospectus, market research, photos of competitors at the show, logo, and corporate colors. If it is at all possible, try to meet with the account executive and the designer so that the designer hears your ideas and not a warmed-over version from the account executive.

2. *Rough sketch.* At this early stage, you will want to see some of the preliminary thinking of the designer. It is not absolutely necessary for him or her to be present, but it helps. As the term implies, the sketches are rough and not polished. Their purpose is to show you the designer's thinking. Listen to all input and digest the design thrust before you say anything. If you are not very good with sketches or blueprints—if it is hard for you to imagine the completed thing from sketches—you might want to skip this stage and go right to the next stage. The purpose of this stage is so that you can get a feel for the direction they will take. (See Fig. 8-7.)

3. *Rendering.* A rendering is a very polished drawing of what the exhibit will look like. (See Fig. 8-8.) It is finished work, which requires a lot of effort. Some people prefer to see just a rendering, because renderings are in full color and show all signage and graphics. Renderings do a good job of indicating exactly what an in-line exhibit will look like. However, some people do not find renderings as useful for island exhibit design because it is difficult to get a feeling for the exhibit from any other angle but the one shown.

4. *White model.* This is a three-dimensional model of the exhibit done to exact scale. It is all white and the purpose of that is for you to see

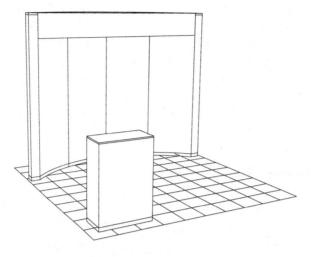

Fig. 8-7. This rough sketch for a portable exhibit was done on a computer-aided design system. Skyline Displays, Inc.

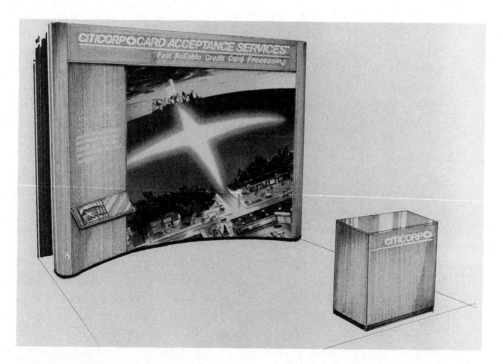

Fig. 8-8. Renderings are full-color, completely finished drawings. Citicorp Card Acceptance Services

the dimensional design and traffic flow. A white model is usually done for an extensive custom exhibit project.

5. *Full graphics model.* Just as its name indicates, the full graphics model will give you an exact impression of what your new exhibit will look like, in full color. When viewing either of these two types of models, be sure to get down on the same level as the visitor entering the exhibit. The easiest way to do this is to put the exhibit up on a stand on top of the desk and then sit with your eye at visitors' eye level.

6. *Fly through.* If you are involved with a very large custom exhibit project, the exhibit house might do a video of the full graphics model, taken from the vantage point of the visitor. The impression is

Design Evaluation Checklist.

1. Quick! Look at the design. What does it communicate in five seconds. As a test, show it to someone who is not familiar with your company. Let them look at it for five seconds, then ask for their impressions. Are these impressions harmonious with the tactics you set? What could make the exhibit design better support those tactics?

2. Look at your image objectives. How does this design meet them? How could it better do so?

3. Look at your sales goals. What elements of the exhibit helps meet them? How could it better do so?

4. What will the overall lighting effect be once the exhibit is in place on the show floor?

5. How does the exhibit inform? Does it clearly state who you are? What you do? How you can help your target audience? Does it use color, pattern, and texture to inform? How might it better do so?

6. If you are using a theme, is it integrated properly into the exhibit design? If it is a corporate theme, does it have prominence in the exhibit? If it is a product theme, is it secondary to the corporate message?

7. Check these items for best use of color, pattern, and shape:

- Signage
- Graphics
- Product displays
- Sales aids

8. Do all activity centers provide a well-equipped, neutral color area for the work they were intended?

9. Do one last continuity check on the overall impression you get from the color scheme, the patterns, and textures, and the shapes used to define space and move the eye around. How could they be better?

Fig. 8-9. You can use this short questionnaire to evaluate your exhibit design project.

eerily that of the visitor walking into the exhibit and is an excellent way to review the new exhibit. Fly throughs are exciting.

No doubt, design is an exciting element of exhibiting and the new exhibit project can be one of the most exciting events in any organization. It is also one of the single most expensive things that a company can purchase, and as such, it is no place for company politics. It is the place for as much input as you can get and cool, calm, and collected sound judgment.

The guidelines here on design, color, form, etc. will be useful for both your original planning of the new exhibit structure and evaluating proposed design solutions. Also, go over the design evaluation checklist in Fig. 8-9 as a reminder of all the design elements you must consider.

9

Successful Show Promotions

THE MEMORY OF A SUCCESSFUL SHOW PROMOTION LASTS YEARS, EVEN decades. It breaks through the clutter of the other messages at the show and captures our undivided attention. We get so involved with a good promotion that only later do we marvel at its cleverness. It has punch, drama, and staying power.

Better still, a great promotion tells us more about the company and the products than we would be willing to learn if mere facts were recited to us. A good promotion sells to us at a deeper level, and we love every minute of it.

Approaching a booth at a trade show, I saw a crowd of about 150 people spilling out from the once neat rows of directors chairs, now standing well into the aisles. On the stage was a Barbara Walters look-alike drawing raucous laughter from the crowd. The master of ceremonies quizzed Ba-Ba Wa-Wa about the company's product. The answers came fast and funny. The attendees loved it. To top it off, just before the close, Ba-Ba gave away the product to the cheering crowd.

This promotion was the hit of the show and ranked as one of the year's 10 most memorable exhibits. Show attendees were overheard asking each other if they had seen what was going on in that company's booth and as the show progressed, the crowds continued to grow. This promotion took place a number of years ago and to those who were there, its memory is as fresh as yesterday. Good promotions have staying power because they are exciting and imaginative. But how can you use promotions like this?

In this chapter, you'll explore the four steps to building successful promotions using the USP, the Unique Selling Proposition, which is the aspect of your product or service that makes it unique, unusual, and set apart from the rest. It is the cornerstone to great promotions. Then, using brainstorming techniques, you'll learn how to turn the USP into a creative strategy that achieves the results you want. Next, you'll get tips on using various media such as advertising, public relations, and direct mail to complete your promotional plans. Finally, you'll learn how to choose, and use, giveaways in your promotions, which is just too valuable a tool for you not to use.

Promotions: what's in it for you?

Of the many things that promotions do for your company, two of the most valuable are that they bring many people to you and that they bring the right people to you. When you decide not to use promotions, you are depending entirely on show management to bring the right people to your carpet line. But will show management promote the show to the audience that you desire to see? Are there others you might like to reach beyond those show management reaches? Even if show management gets them in the door, how will you get them into your exhibit?

Promotions bring more of the right people into your exhibit. That's why you need promotions, and the thing that makes promotions work is the USP.

Successful promotions using the USP

The concept of the USP, or unique selling proposition, is not a new one. It is, however, a sound one that is especially helpful when creating promotions, whether you are creating them on your own, or with the help of your advertising agency.

There are four steps to creating successful promotions:

1. *Setting objectives*. Do you want leads? Sales? And if so how many? Or do you need to build your image?

2. *Determining the USP*. Identify exactly what sets your product or service apart from the rest. What is unique about it that differentiates it.

3. *Developing the creative strategy*. The creative strategy must be designed to bridge the gap between what you have—the product's USP—and what you want—the objectives. Two important tools to working out the creative strategy are brainstorming and themeing.

4. *Merchandising it everywhere*. Your creative strategy can be leveraged to the maximum only if you use the theme as often as possible throughout the show, only if you merchandise it.

Step 1: setting objectives

The first step to good promotions is to identify your objectives. Provided you did the work outlined in Chapter 7 on planning, this should be easy. Remember, you can only have one primary objective, so you must choose between building your image or getting leads/sales. Even if you choose leads/sales as your primary objective, you will also be working on your image as well. Likewise, when image is what you are after, there will be visitors who have specific product questions and needs. No matter, one objective must still clearly take precedence and drive the promotion.

When setting objectives, be as specific as possible. If you desire leads, be sure to state how many and for which product. Let's continue with our example from chapter 7 of the Mailing Systems Company. In that example, the company's objective was lead gathering. It specifically stated that the trade show program for the Mailing Systems Company needed to deliver 1,000 leads. Assuming that five shows would be attended, each show would need to generate 200 leads. Similarly, your objective should be just as specific. If your objective is to build your image, be just as specific. Are you building your image as a progressive company? A service-driven company? A leader?

Step 2: determining the USP

Step 2 should be the simplest of all because you should already know what sets your product or service apart from the rest of the competition. Why do those who buy your product prefer it to others? Does it cost less? Does it do something the other's don't? Is it better looking? Is it the most expensive? Does it need less service, or is the service better?

Exhibitors with commodity products often find that there is little to set them apart and that, honestly, there is nothing unique about their product. If this describes your products, try focusing on their best attribute, making the case for it as strong as possible; then use the promotion to add the excitement that is not inherent of your product.

Step 3: developing creative strategy

Step 3 is the most challenging—and the most fun. If you like solving puzzles and thinking with the creative side of your right brain, then this is for you. If not, then it's time to turn the work over to those who are good at it, like your advertising or promotions agency.

The creative strategy bridges the gap between what you have and what you want. For example, the Mailing Systems Company's objective is 200 leads per show for their high-priced mailing centers, which can cost as much as $15,000. Their USP is their high price and quality image. Arriving at the USP is as simple as that. To bridge the gap between the USP and their objectives, of 200 leads for high-end mailing systems they decided to do a mailing prior to the show that offers 300 key decision makers a complementary brass business card case, engraved with their initials. The mailing included a return card on which the prospect indicates the initials to be engraved on the case. Cases would be picked up, the mailer states, by appointment in the exhibit at the show.

Not only did this creative strategy bridge the gap between their objectives and USP, they kept their target audience to a manageable number as well as hand selecting their target audience for their sales staff. The premium offered has a high perceived value and is personalized. The target then comes to the exhibit, by appointment, to pick up the gift, thereby ensuring that an appropriate staffer is on hand to give them a personal tour of the booth.

How can you come up with a creative strategy? Brainstorming is a highly effective technique for creative thinking.

Brainstorming techniques and tips

The following brainstorming techniques are designed to get your creative juices flowing:

Never say no.   One of the basic rules of brainstorming is that all ideas have merit. Something said in jest or that might sound absurd could have merit an hour later. Never say no to any idea. Consider all ideas. It will ensure that the ideal mill of your mind doesn't shut down. A sure way to shut it down is for someone to tell you that your last idea was no good.

Write it down.   Writing down each idea serves two separate purposes, both important. First, it gives validity to all ideas, even the silly or small ones—and that keeps the ideas coming. Second, it is a way to record all thoughts for later reference and refinement. One idea leads to another which triggers yet a third, and so on.

Set parameters.   This tip is important. You will get the very best results from your brainstorming if you take pains to define what you are brainstorming about. It is too broad a topic to simply say that you are brainstorming to get a great idea for the upcoming show. It is a better brainstorming technique to state that you are trying to find a promotional plan to get 200 key decision makers into the booth, using the USP of high quality. This way, you have set specific parameters of the target audience and the USP.

Use flip charts and color markers.   Write the parameters of the brainstorming—like the target, your objectives, and the USP—on one flip chart and tape it to the wall so that it can easily be seen throughout the session. Also, write all of the ideas on other flip charts and tape those to the wall as they are filled so that they can trigger other ideas.

Recap and synthesize.   When the rate of ideas slows down dramatically, it's time to stop and recap. After the recap, solicit new ideas. If there are none, then the session is over and it's time to do the final recap. Review the ideas again, this time eliminating the outlandish. Then start to synthesize by asking other staffers to discuss their favorite concepts. Try to bring forth the outstanding and feasible ideas.

Reaching your audience

At some shows, you can attract many visitors and get many leads. Here the reach is broad and the results are broad. At other shows, you might attract many visitors and get just a few leads. Here the reach is still broad while the results can be said to be narrow. At still other times, you might want to be able to attract just a few visitors but be able to take leads from a high proportion of those you attract. This time, both the reach and results are narrow. The scope of the reach and the results can, and should, be anticipated in advance as part of your promotional strategy and be a parameter of your brainstorming. Table 9-1 can help you see how this concept of size of show audience versus size of your target audience can be a factor in your promotional plans.

Setting promotional reach parameters

The audience size that you need to reach in order to get the results you desire is a very important factor in developing your promotional plans. First, consider the size of the audience you need to reach to get the results you desire. For example, do you need to reach large numbers of people to get to a very few because the few are not presently known to you? Or is it possible to pinpoint your target audience? Or is it a mass communications job that needs to be done so you will be reaching a large mass in order to get your message across to all of that large audience.

This relationship between the size of the reach of your promotional efforts versus the size of your target audience can, and does, affect how you do your promotions and can even help you anticipate some of the problems you will run into. Table 9-1 compares and contrasts the three promotional reach situations and should further aid you in setting brainstorming parameters.

As you can see in the table, there are three ways to look at the audience you must attract in order to make the targeted contacts you need. In the first situation, you must attract a mass of people to get your results, which center on influencing that whole audience. This is often used when an exhibitor needs to educate a market or get the word out on a new product—all at once. In this situation, reaching the total audience prior to the show is not critical. Reaching them at the show, however, can be very important if you are to make an immediate impact upon them. If you miss them at the show,

Table 9-1.
Comparing Promotional Parameters

	Wide/Wide	Wide/Narrow	Narrow/Narrow
Attract:	Mass audience	Mass audience	Individuals
To Reach:	Mass audience	Individuals	Individuals
Preshow:	Not critical	Not critical	Critical
Promotions:	Any mass media can be used because mass media is effective		Direct mail
At show:	Important, but not critical. Can reach them after the show using mass media.		Critical. If miss them at the show, it is hard
Incentives:	Not important	Important	Very important
Message:	Entertaining	Filters	Informs
Problems:	Getting them to take action	Getting enough through the filter	Enough people in target?

all is not lost. You can follow up the show with some mass marketing by way of ads or direct mail and still reach them.

For example, early in its life, Apple Computer, Inc. caught the imagination of the entire market by offering free passes to Disneyland the year that a major industry show was held in Anaheim. Their objective was to get the word out and raise awareness so that people would stop saying, "Apple who?" This promotion, designed to reach the masses did just that. Their exhibit was packed all day and up to an hour after the show closed.

Often, a mass appeal promotion will include a live presentation rather than a giveaway, such as Apple did. The problem to consider in the Wide/Wide reach situation is measuring your image objective.

An example of the second situation using a mass approach to get a specific individuals, or the Wide/Narrow reach, can best be described as looking for a needle in a haystack. Pre-show and at-show promotions, as well as premiums, can all be used effectively. For example, Dupont sought to feature Cromalin, their well-known system for proofing four-color work prior to its being printed. Their theme was a simple but clever one. Cromalin gives an exact duplicate of the finished printed piece, therefore, it is a clone of the printed piece thus, the origins of their theme was born featuring an ice cream *clone*.

The preshow promotion, literature on hand in the exhibit and the exhibit graphis all included their giveaway, which could be seen all over the show floor. A raspberry and pistachio ice cream cone. (See Fig.-9.1.) Attendees lined up in great numbers to get the cones and while they were in

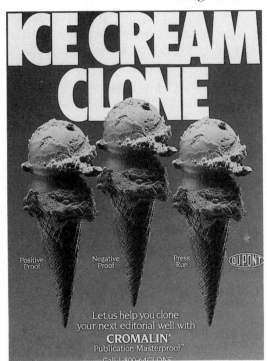

Fig. 9-1. Example of a Wide/Narrow promotional reach. Dupont's Cromalin Ice Cream Clone mailer.

line, staffers talked with them and qualified them. Dupont used this mass promotion to filter out of the total audience a few individuals who had an interest in press proofing systems. The ice cream cone giveaway brought plenty of people to the booth who were then filtered by the staffers who chatted with those in line waiting for their cones.

In the third situation, the promotional effort is targeted to a smaller audience within which even smaller numbers of prospects are found. The classic example of this is the previously mentioned exhibitor who mailed an offer of a free business card case to a very select list of key prospects. In this situation, the highly targeted preshow mailing is critical.

Using themes

The *Advertising Manager's Handbook*, Dartnel, defines a theme in this way:

> "A theme is an absolute essential. It is the theme which transforms a random assortment of individual ads into a cohesive, unified whole, making a neat, logical package. The theme, however, is not the suject of either the campaign or any individual ad. . . ."

While the reference here is to advertising, this definition of the theme also applies to trade shows. Themes, defined as a strong central idea, have been used for decades to express the delivery of a strategic marketing concept to the target audience with impact. While many trendy marketing concepts have come and left us, the use of the theme remains.

Themes take on special dimensions when they are used at trade shows because of the unique ability of shows to encompass all of the marketing communications media available. Trade shows are the perfect opportunity for themes to be carried out through all of the media, from the exhibit design, advertising, to billboards.

As the *Advertising Handbook* also states, "Themes are deceptively simple. They look easy to create. Most, however, came into being only after company marketing people and their agency counterparts racked their brains for countless hours." Themes have two functions. First, they link the USP to the market by slanting the USP to the market. An example of USP slant would be to feature highly favorable research results to technically oriented decision makers. By focusing on research results, the high quality of the product or its performance is brought to light. In this way, the theme tells the target more, faster than taking the conventional route of explaining product features and benefits or solutions.

In the example of the mailing systems company, the theme might be "Solid gold quality." The theme could be carried out in preshow advertising as the main headline in testimonial ads featuring research, in the exhibit along with the brass card case give away, and by having a drawing for a solid gold card case. The theme could also dictate the color scheme of the booth and any printed materials, like invitations to the suite. (See Fig. 9-2.) Themes often revolve around these concepts:

- New product release
- Cost savings
- Unique feature/benefit
- Time savings
- Reliability
- Service and support
- Testimonial, research
- Case study

The second aspect of the theme is to bring the audience closer to taking an action. The desired action is usually a decision. The theme should work to get visitors motivated and show them what the next step might be. Not all themes have this call to action as a strong enough part of their message but, at the least, it should be implicit if not explicit.

Step 4: Merchandise it everywhere

Now that you have set your objectives, determined the USP, and developed a creative strategy using brainstorming and have a theme, it's time to write up

Fig. 9-2. This theme, centering on the truck giveaway, was carried over from the national Square D advertising campaign. Courtesy Square D.

a promotional plan. The key to having a powerful presence at a trade show is to have that theme touch as many aspects of the show as possible, that is, to merchandise it everywhere.

It is helpful to think of the experience the attendee will have as you plan the promotional campaign. Consider the number of times she is likely to be exposed to your message. Figure 9-3 is a Promotional Opportunities Checklist, which identifies for you the times when your message can reach the target audience.

Once you have identified the number of occasions at which you can expose the theme to your audience, then you can select the media you will use. Sometimes a brainstorming session will identify the media, as can the nature of the promotion. In brainstorming sessions, someone might have suggested mailing a premium or premium offer to a select audience or running an ad to a broader audience. In these cases, the media selection comes as a result of the brainstorming session.

On the other hand, the selection of media could be determined by the type of promotion you desire. For example, preshow promotions are limited to direct mail, advertising, and to a very limited extent, telemarketing. Public relations just doesn't fit easily into preshow promotional plans because of the lack of control over timing.

Promotional Opportunities Checklist

	Yes	No
1. How will attendees get your message prior to the show? Can you use advertising, direct mail, or telemarketing?	____	____
2. Will attendees see your message once they get to the show site, the hotel, or on the way there? Can you use in-flight advertising or billboards at the airport in taxicabs or along the main route from the airport to the hotels?	____	____
3. If attendees will drive to the show, can you reach them on radio?	____	____
4. Will attendees be able to see anything about you at the hotel, such as a closed-circuit television channel you can advertise on?	____	____
5. Did your promotional plans include an incentive or premium that will motivate attendees to find you and visit your exhibit?	____	____
6. Did your promotions state the location of the exhibit, especially if it is away from the main traffic flow?	____	____
7. Will your exhibit catch attendees attention as they walk down the aisle? Does it include attention-getting techniques, color, motion, or sound?	____	____
8. What will bring attendees into your booth? Are the staffers briefed as to how the promotion will work and are they ready to assist by facilitating entry of visitors into the exhibit?	____	____
9. What will keep attendees there? Is the promotion simple, easy to do, and fun, and is there a reasonable probability that attendees will be successful when participating in it?	____	____

Fig. 9-3. Promotional opportunities checklist.

At-show promotions lend themselves to other media, such as showlike daily advertising, local morning broadcasts and cable, billboards, and under-the-hotel door stuffers.

Tips on using the media

Once you have decided on the media you will use, it's time to put what you know about advertising, direct mail, etc. into action, or to call an agency. The follows are tips on using various media at trade shows.

Advertising. The simplest thing to do with your ads is to place an additional line at the bottom of those you are now running to say something like, "See us at the XYZ Show, Booth 1234." This is easy to do because all you have to do is call the publication's production department and tell them what you want. For a small fee, usually well under $50, they will add the line to your ad a month or two before the show.

The impact of this type of tag line is not impressive, so if you really want your audience to sit up and take notice, then you need to think about running an ad that features your theme. These are the most powerful aids in getting the attention of your audience. (See Fig. 9-4.)

Because Of The Growing Interest In Ethyl's Capabilities, There Haven't Been This Many People Trying To Get Into One Booth Since 1955.

The Ethyl Molded Products, Ethyl Bromine Chemicals and Ethyl Industrial Chemicals Divisions have all put their heads together to create a plastics exhibit that's sure to be one of the more popular booths at the NPE '88.

Some people will come to hear about Ethyl Industrial Chemicals' antioxidants, like Ethanox® 330 hindered phenolic. And about development of the exciting new Ethanox 398 fluorophosphite.

Some will want to learn more about Ethyl brominated flame retardants like Saytex® 102, the largest selling flame retardant in the nation.

And others will want to see what's new at Ethyl Molded Products, the largest tool maker and manufacturer of custom injection-molded plastic components in the U.S.

But everybody who sticks their head into our booth will see that Ethyl is one company that knows this industry from the bottom up; from the molecular design of chemical additives to the complete manufacture of finished products.

So come see us this year at booth 3400. If for some reason you can't squeeze in, write: Manager, Corporate Advertising, Ethyl Corporation, P. O. Box 2448, Richmond, VA 23218.

Ethyl

See Ethyl In Booth 3400 At NPE '88.

Ethanox and Saytex are registered trademarks of Ethyl Corporation.† 1988 Ethyl Corporation.

Fig. 9-4. This ad was created especially for preshow advertising. Ethyl Corporation.

Direct mail.   Selecting the right list is the key to effective direct mail campaigns. The best lists are:

1. *Pre-registrants*, provided they can be had with only your target audience, such as without exhibitors.
2. *Last year's registrants*, if the show stays in the same location or is an association show.
3. *The association membership list.*
4. *Your sales force's key prospect list.*
5. *Geographic and title selected lists* from a publications' circulation list.

Public Relations.   The key to public relations at trade shows is to understand that the vast majority of the press will be at the major shows you go to and that this provides a wonderful opportunity for you. You can tap into it three ways. First, prior to the show, call and write to the press people that you wish to see at the show. Inquire if they will be there and ask if they could set aside some time to see whatever it is that you have that is new. Remember, they are in the news business and are only interested in what is new, so keep focused on that when you talk to them.

The second way to tap the power of the press is to have a good press kit for them when they come into the exhibit. Again, keep the information news-worthy and eliminate fluff. While you can leave your press kit in the press room, you will also want to keep a supply of them in the booth for the editors and writers with whom you have made an appointment.

The third way to make an impact is to follow up with them after the show to be sure that their questions are answered and to provide any missing data. This way, you'll be sure that your message is breaking through the clutter of the show to reach your important press contacts.

Telemarketing.   The very best way to use telemarketing is to call key prospects or customers to inquire if they are going to the show and to make an appointment with them for a private consultation or demonstration.

Keeping promotions on schedule

The trouble with promotions is that they are time-consuming, and unless you simply turn it over to an agency, you are apt to not allow enough time for all of the work that needs to be done. Here is a typical promotions schedule that you should use as a guideline to your thinking when planning promotions.

Five months before the show:

- Conduct brainstorming session
- Decide on theme to be used
- Establish promotional plan to identify all promotional opportunities
- Select media to be used

Four months before the show:

- Fix budget for each media project.
- Select the following
  ~Direct mail lists
  ~Publications for ads
  ~Key press people
  ~Prospect list for telemarketing
- Turn these over to the agency:
  ~Outline of promotional plan, budget, theme
  ~Media selections (above)

Three months before the show:

- Review from agency:
  ~Ad layout
  ~Direct mail campaign
  ~Press kit draft copy
  ~Telemarketing script

Two months before the show

- Place advertising space and send materials
- Print direct mail materials
- Send pre-show press packet to press.

One month before the show:

- Run advertising
- Mail direct mail so that the last mailing arrives on the attendees desk the week prior to the show.
- Call editors to schedule meetings.
- Do telemarketing.

Giveaways: how to choose them, how to use them

Every exhibitor dreams of having just the right giveaway that will make the attendees go wild in the aisles. Most, however, settle for premiums that lack imagination and do little to help reach sales goals. It's easy to give examples of those that don't work, like most key chains, luggage tags, and buttons. These items quickly turn into junk in the back of a drawer or get tossed in the trash because they have a low perceived value. If a premium is to work, it needs to have a high perceived value or contain useful information.

The best way to get a premium that will work for you is to include the challenge of coming up with a premium as part of your brainstorming session. By starting with the objectives, you will more easily see options for creative premium solutions. It also helps if you center your thinking around the theme and have the premium tie in to it. Here are some examples of premiums that were successful for other exhibitors. (See Fig. 9-5.)

- Trail nut mix for a cable health network.
- Cholesterol testing from the manufacturer of the test equipment. (See Fig. 9-6.)
- Pocket guide to printing from a paper manufacturer.
- Gold plated bookmark from a company that does metal plating.
- Toy robot from a robotics firm.
- Swiss chocolates from a company importing a major new product from Switzerland.
- Emery boards from an airfreight firm having a similar sounding name.
- Stress cards from a psychiatric hospital.

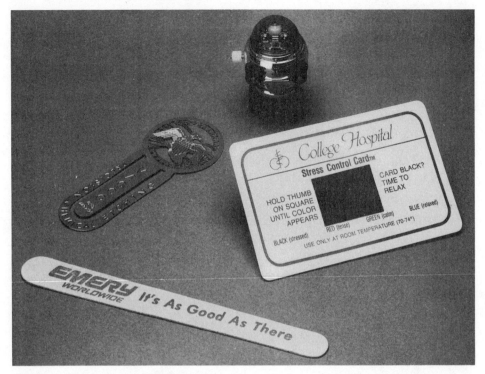

Fig. 9-5. Premiums that worked.

Fig. 9-6. This medical diagnostic equipment company offered a complimentary cholesterol test as its giveaway.

Fig. 9-7. This Marilyn Monroe look-alike was used to distribute premiums. Although quite a crowd gathered to see her, no one spoke to this exhibitors' staffers.

Fig. 9-8. These attorneys register for the tee-shirt offer. The tee-shirt reads, "Doctor, Lawyer, Indian Chief." Each title had a check box and the one for "Lawyer" had a big red check mark. The registration card is a filter, and only selected visitors are offered a mini demo.

In each of these examples, it is easy to see the relationship between the item given away and the exhibitor giving it away—and that's what makes a great advertising specialty item. (See Fig. 9-7) one that didn't work.)

The worst way to use premiums is to put them in a basket or dish on a table or the aisle for anyone to grab. The better way to use them is for opening conversations or closing them. In either case, staffers should be instructed that they are not to think of their main task in the exhibit as giving out premiums. Instead, the premiums are there as a tool to be used to get the interest level of the passers-by up a notch. (See Fig. 9-8.)

The big guns

As you have seen in this chapter, promotions can be the big gun you are looking for to outmaneuver the competition and leapfrog to the head of the market. They are fun to dream up, and if you are the creative type, you will probably be able to come up with more ideas than you can use. Just remember two things. Always keep one eye on your objective because that will prevent you from getting carried away in the excitement of it. Don't be afraid to try anything. If it doesn't work, you'll try something else next year.

10

Selling at trade shows

THIS CHAPTER IS ARGUABLY THE MOST IMPORTANT ONE IN THE BOOK. IF YOU don't have much time to devote to trade shows and are only able to turn your attentions to one aspect, this is the one to go after. Similarly, if you have very limited financial resources but want to increase the number of leads you get from every show you go to, start here.

What kind of pay-off can you expect after putting into place and working with the information here? Plenty. Typically, our clients, after working with this same information, see a doubling or even tripling of the leads they get from shows over their previous performance. The potential for payoff is large—if you're willing to work on it. And the particularly attractive aspect is that you can do this without spending one more dime.

If you have any sales experience at all, you will find this material super easy. Even if you don't, you can master it by spending just a few minutes on each of the exercises included here. Regardless of whether you have previous sales experience or not, exhibit selling is not brain surgery, and you should feel free to have fun with it and enjoy trying out new approaches and gambits in the practice sessions before the show and even in the exhibit.

If you do have a sales background, don't feel that you should automatically know this information. Very few selling skills courses address the esoteric aspects of selling from an exhibit. Even so, it won't take you very long to adjust your own selling style and put the special "spin" on it required for exhibit selling. It's all very logical and common-sense based.

In this chapter, we'll start by covering the five big rules of the trade show road, which will keep you immune from committing any faux pas when you work the exhibit. From there, we'll explore the basics of non-verbal communications as they apply to trade shows. Finally, and importantly, we will explore the four selling skills: 1) welcoming the visitor and starting a conversation; 2) qualifying to quickly uncover need; 3) responding to the need; and 4) gaining consensus on the next step to take and writing up the order or, more likely, the lead.

The five big rules of the road

Trade shows have a sort of etiquette all their own. There are acceptable and decidedly unacceptable behaviors. For example, it is not acceptable to sit (unless your leg is in a cast or you are in a wheelchair). It is expected that you will refrain from smoking, even if you smoke and your visitor lights up. It is expected that very early on in the conversation, you will try to find out, as quickly and efficiently as possible, exactly what the visitor needs. So that you don't end up looking like you don't know what you're doing, take a few minutes to review these Five Big Rules of the Trade Show Road. If they just seem like common sense to you, you have good instincts. Just be sure you aren't relying on those instincts alone to tell you what's right and wrong. Double check by taking a very close look at this list. A full explanation of each one will follow.

1. *Be available.* Stand with good proximity to the aisle or main traffic flow through or near your exhibit.
2. *Be warm.* Smile and make eye contact. Use an open stance.
3. *Don't offend.* No smoking, drinking, eating, or chewing gum.
4. *Make a positive impression.* Dress upscale of your audience. Keep it neat. Place your badge on the right, the side of your body that comes forward when you shake hands, making it easier to see and read.
5. *Be pro-active.* Take responsibility for engaging the visitor in conversation, finding out what he or she needs. And be responsible for the quality of their experience in your exhibit.

As you can see, the issue is one of quality. Each of the Big Five is there to enhance the quality of the visitor's time with you. In very few other selling situations will your prospect leave your presence and, within a minute and a half, be in the presence of your competitor. At trade shows, that happens all the time and you need to be ready for it by looking and acting better than the competition. This is not the time to offend because you won't have time

Fig. 10-1. These staffers have set up the physical barrier of the tables and the psychological barrier of the phone and the newspaper.

to recover. Now, let's look at each of the Big Five to discover how they will make you more competitive on the show floor.

Be available

The more available you are to the attendees, the easier it is to invite them into your exhibit. Position yourself with close proximity to the aisle so that you can easily make eye contact with them. If your exhibit is a large one and traffic flows naturally into it, don't block that flow, but stand next to it. Figure 10-1 shows two staffers breaking rule 1.

One of the major behaviors to avoid is staffers talking to each other. There are two reasons for this. First, when staffers talk to each other, they cannot talk to visitors. Second, visitors are likely to interrupt staffers engaged in conversation. The productivity of even the largest and most well-run exhibits is greatly diminished by staffers talking to each other. It's a habit that is very easy to fall into and very very difficult to break.

Be warm

Being warm means using an open stance, one that doesn't close out the visitor (see Fig. 10-2). How to stand is covered further in this chapter on nonverbal communications. But for now, keep in mind that your stance should be open. Equally important is a warm, genuine smile. Arrange your face as though you are glad to see the visitor. Tell him or her through your eyes that it pleases you that he or she stopped by. Be careful that your smile doesn't look pasted on, especially when you are tired. When you feel as though you are forcing your smile, it's time for a break.

Fig. 10-2. The home base stance is open and invites professionalism and availability.

Don't offend

Not offending means not smoking, drinking, or eating in the exhibit. But that's not all. Don't look bored either. It might be a bit difficult to be and look genuinely fascinated by the 100th time you've listened to the same customer problems, but analyze it from the customer's point of view. This is only the first time he's told it. Again, keep fresh and be attentive. (See Fig. 10-3.) And of course, anyone who has worked more than one show knows to keep a roll of breath mints in their pocket.

Make a positive impression

Your company should have a dress code for staffers working in an exhibit, even if it's only a simple policy statement like, "conservative business attire," and you're quite sure everyone knows exactly what that means. Increasingly, exhibitors will take the opportunity offered by trade shows to strategize what the staffers will wear so that it too makes a competitive statement. One exhibitor at a major construction show had all the staffers wear grey pinstripes to put forth a big, powerful, conservative image. Another exhibitor, whose position as the revolutionaries in their market, encourage their staffers to add a spot of bright color such as a bright yellow tie or pocket scarf or blouse to keep them memorable and to underscore their individualistic ap-

Fig. 10-3. How many things is this disgusting staffer doing wrong?

proach. You, too, need to think through your dress code and have it help, not hinder, your overall approach.

Don't forget to place your badge on the right side of your body to make it easier for visitors to read. As noted before, that is the part of your body that comes forward when you shake hands. Another way to help your staffers stand out in the crowd is to give them custom badges. Any trophy shop can make them for you for under $4 each. Custom name tags will help identify your staffers and make them much easier for visitors to locate.

Be proactive

Being proactive is the "biggie" that makes you really stand out from the competition. Most exhibitors stand around waiting for someone to come over and talk to them. They are reminiscent of museum guards, waiting for someone to ask a question. If you want to out-pace the competition, then get your staffers to understand that *they* need to make it easy—not difficult—for visitors to come talk to them. Staffers must realize that they, not the visitors, should be doing the work. Make it easy for visitors to be with you, not your competitor.

If you want to evaluate your own team on the show floor, judge them by these five rules. Then go take a look at your competitors, and ask yourself who is making the best impression on your prospects.

Perfecting nonverbal communication

Your body speaks before you say a word. You know that, but have you ever thought about how nonverbal communications might be different in an exhibit? First, you will be using your entire body because you are standing, not sitting as most people are in daily business situations. Second, the trade show environment is very public, and every motion and gesture, no matter how slight, is a public one.

Most of us use upper body nonverbals in our daily business communications, and we're quite good at both reading and sending signals. We know when a prospect is bored because we see her start to fidget with the things on her desk. All of this changes at trade shows where our home bases—our work surface, our lap, and the ability to prop up our head and touch our faces with our hands—are lost. So what should we do with our hands when we're standing in an exhibit?

The answer is simple: anything that looks powerful and open. Stuffing them both in your pockets doesn't. Neither does folding them across your chest or midsection. If you have ever taken a presentation skills course, you're already familiar with the "home base" position illustrated in Fig. 10.4. This, or any other powerful gestures, are what you are looking for.

Consider that, even though these gestures might feel uncomfortable or even slightly overdone, they look appropriate in the exhibit. This is because, on the scale of business communications, exhibit communications lies somewhere between a one-on-one presentation and the group presentation. It is more public, more formal than a similar presentation done in the office. Therefore, you need to select a stance and use gestures somewhat more formal than those you use daily.

Four steps to successful trade show selling

There are four skills used to communicate and get the job done for exhibitors around the world. These skills should change and take on different dimensions depending on the culture of the buyers, the culture of the seller, the type of show, the audience, the market, the product, and even your own corporate culture. Here we will consider a typical skills set (grouping of skills) commonly used in North America. Generally, U.S. skills are slightly more fast-paced than those used in Canada. The specific spin on skills, however, can be dependent on other factors such as regional ethnocentricies as well. For example, skills used at Toronto shows are most like those used in Boston than either are to local shows in the deep South. As you read the rest of this chapter, consider how to put that special slant on your selling skills so that they'll work the very best they can in your situation.

Fig. 10-4. Two staffers, both using the home base stance, are busy observing visitor types before welcoming them to the exhibit.

Successful trade show selling skills require customizing and personalizing. No two staffers have the same personality and just as staffers are different, so too should what they say be different. Pat phrases won't do here. Each staffer must take time to think about how he or she would like to handle each of the four skills and exactly what they will say to visitors.

If you are serious about getting the very, very most you can from your trade show investment, you'll insist that your staffers actually rehearse these four steps or skills, especially the first, welcoming visitors. By practicing the skills before they get to the exhibit, they avoid warming up with real prospects. And if they are productive right from the start, they will immediately go after visitors, turning them into leads as soon as the show opens.

Here is a quick look at the four selling skills most commonly used in trade show exhibits. If you are at all familiar with any of the "stepped" selling systems so popular here in the United States, this one will come easy to you. If not, think of yourself as the visitor as you read and imagine how helpful it is to have the staffers in the exhibits you visit use this system to lead you through uncovering your need and filling it. When staffers use a stepped selling system like this one, visitors are more easily helped and their satisfaction level is higher. However, to completely ensure visitor satisfaction, as with any selling system, the four-step structure must eventually be left in the background and the visitor and their need should occupy the foreground. The visitor, not the four-step structure, drives the interaction.

Fig. 10-5 is a quick reference guide to the four sales skills used at trade shows. Take a moment now to review them. Although they seem simple, don't make the mistake of underestimating this process. It's like a golf swing or fly-fishing cast: less is more. To be able to execute each of the steps with elegant simplicity is to make it look easy to all who watch. And all who watch invariably underestimate what it takes to do it right.

Step 1: welcoming the visitor.	From the very first moments, take control of the quality of the visitor's experience. Start by making it easy for them to be there. Open a conversation with them and don't make them work to open the conversation with you. Watch their nonverbal communication for clues to their level of interst.
Step 2: qualifying visitors and uncovering needs.	After welcoming the visitor and engaging them in conversation, start to get to know them and their need. Use classic opening probes like who, what, where, when, and why. The objective is to find out in about three minutes what they think they need. Prioritize your qualifying questions so that if the visitor decides to terminate the conversation for whatever reason, you have covered the important questions.
Step 3: Presenting the needs fulfillment solution.	Next, respond to the need that was uncovered during Step 2, qualify. As you let them know that you have what they are looking for, and as you present your needs fulfillment solution, continue to focus on the visitor, not your product or service. This should be easy if you have done a good job of qualifying to uncover that need. Be warned that even the best exhibit staffers fall into the trap of simply "pitching" the product and not keeping the visitor in mind.
Step 4: Closing and commitment.	At this point in the interaction, your objective is twofold. First, you and the visitor need to agree on a desired next step and bring the interaction to a close. The discussion is brought to a conclusion when you assure them of a follow-up action—someone will call or literature will be sent—and thank them for having spent time with you. Last, write up the lead and be sure all the qualifying data has been captured. Better yet, take notes during your conversation.

Fig. 10-5. Quick reference guide to exhibit selling skills.

Welcoming the visitor

Welcoming the visitor is where it all starts and ends if welcoming skills aren't done right. Most staffers, if they think about this aspect of exhibit selling at all, view it in terms of wondering what they should say to passers-by. Their emphasis is all wrong. Instead, you need to be busy watching the visitors and carefully observing what they do so that you can extract information from their behavior. Let their behavior tell you what to say to them. When you do this, you will be reacting very naturally and comfortably to them—not worrying about what you're going to say to them.

Take a moment now and respond to the visitors actions described here. Visualize them walking into or near your exhibit and react naturally to their presence. Your first instinct is probably right. There are no "right" answers here, just possible ways to answer. The following are some suggestions for talking to each visitor type, however:

Visitor A: the active visitors

- Respond to their interest with interest. For example, "I see you are very interested in our meters. Can you tell me about your interest in them?"

- If they ask you a question, give the shortest answer possible, and within the answer, ask them a question. Here's an example of an answer to a question about price. "The price varies depending on model, number of options, and quantity. If you tell me a bit more about your situation, I'll be in a better position to give you a realistic range. How would you use them and how many would you need?"

  Although most salespeople are already familiar with this technique of using a question to answer a question, it has special significance at trade shows because the only visitors likely to start off asking you questions are either very serious prospects or competitors. In either case, a red flag should go up, putting you on alert.

Visitor B: the curious visitor

- Although this visitor's interested gaze is coming your way, they are just curious and not yet committed to spending time with you. If you can, move them into the exhibit as soon as possible.

- One approach is to take a step or two forward and say, "Welcome to our exhibit. Are you familiar with us?" If you are facile and can handle it, this closed-end question can lead somewhere instead of nowhere. If the visitor says no, then you ask if they use the products you sell, and listen for the response. If the visitor says yes, then the staffer can either ask in what context or simply offer a tour of the booth or if the visitor would like to see what's new. (See Fig. 10-6.)

Fig. 10-6. Staffer welcomes the curious visitor on the aisle and engages him in conversation.

- Take a step forward and ask how they are finding this year's show and is it suiting their needs. The appropriate follow-up questioning gambit that should be used here uncovers their needs.
- The approach to Visitor B, who is only mildly curious about you, is to use that moment of curiosity to build real interest.

Visitor C: the passive visitors

- Visitor C has simply made eye contact with you. No more or less. It would be inappropriate to come on like "gang busters" with product talk or offers of tours of the booth.
- Slow and easy is the approach here. Try the social icebreakers to get them to slow down and chat.
- Once they are talking, move up to the same type of suggestions for Visitor B, above.

Staffers should always immediately approach Type A, Active Visitors. If your staffers are missing Active Visitors, they simply aren't doing a very proficient job and are wasting your trade show dollars. (See Fig. 10-7.) If there aren't enough "A" visitors to your exhibit to keep staffers busy all of the time,

Fig. 10-7. This visitor is an "A" and actively looks at product literature . . . but where are the staffers?

then they should go after "B" visitors. When traffic is slow, they can avoid boredom by engaging the "C" visitors in conversation. In that way your staffers will be operating in the most productive manner.

A practical aspect of staffer proficiency is that visitors don't sort themselves out quite so neatly, and a staffer working your booth close to the aisle will find herself standing next to a "B" and a few moments later making eye contact with a "C". Therefore, staffers need to think through precisely what they want to say to each visitor type and practice it so that they can spring into action quickly. If they are slow, productivity is slow.

Also, make sure that staffers make no assumptions about equating visitor type with opportunity. While the "A" visitor might be more aggressive in expressing his or her need, the "B" or "C" visitor might be as good or even better prospect. You'll never know until you take the next step and qualify the visitor.

Qualifying visitors and uncovering needs

Most everyone—especially journalism school grads and sales trainers—is familiar with the "Big W" questions: Who, what, where, when, and why. These are the classic opening probes, so called because they cannot be answered with a "yes" or "no," which closes down the information flow. At trade shows, open probes are used to accomplish the same task as they are in other sales situations to move the sale along. There are, however, two slight differences. First, you must get acquainted with the person you are talking to very quickly and then move on to uncover the need, also quickly. Second, you must prioritize your questions about the need because the visitor can walk away at any time.

Therefore, your first assignment immediately after welcoming the visitor and engaging them in conversation is to find out with whom you are talking. Just about the time that your conversation gets rolling along, you need to bring it to a halt and introduce yourself and meet your visitor, inquiring about his or her name, company, and title. Their show badge will make the task easier and usually provide everything but the title. To get at that, simply ask, "And what is it you do for ABC Electronics?"

If the visitor is missing a badge, beware. Often, competitors will slip their badges in a pocket and go shop the competition. If the visitor standing before you has no badge remember: First "know," then "need." Get to know who they are before spending time with them. If you don't feel comfortable that they are who they say they are, proceed slowly and ask plenty of questions designed to unmask the phoney.

Once you have gotten to "know" your visitor it's time to move on to uncovering their need. Here's where the classic opening probes do their work. What do they think they want? Why do they think they want it? When would they like to start? If you could know just the answers to those questions, plus maybe a question about quantity and budget—how many and how much—you would probably be happily on the way to evaluating this visitor in terms of prospect potential.

There's only one thing standing in your way and that's the visitor's ability to leave you at any time, regardless of whether you have completed qualifying her or not. You must know which questions are more important so you can ask those first.

In field sales situations an account executive might take 40 or 50 minutes to qualify a visitor and uncover need. That luxury of time is simply not available at trade shows. Where the average interaction lasts merely *three to five minutes*. Therefore, if most of your staffers are field sales people, it will be helpful to remind them that they need to shift gears into high speed for qualifying. Research shows that visitors appreciate quick qualification and see it as respectful of their valuable time.

If there is precious little time in the exhibit and the visitor can more on whenever he likes, it makes sense to prioritize the qualifying questions you ask. This is especially true if you attend a conference where there is much competition for the attendees time from social events, seminars, meetings, and plenty of exhibits. In this exercise, you should rearrange this list of classic open probes so that you get the best information first:

Who   —   are you talking to by name and title?
What   —   is their role in deciding about this purchase?

What	—	do they think is their main need?
Where	—	is the delivery location?
Who	—	is this company?
What	—	else do they think they might need?
Why	—	does this visitor feel he/she needs this solution?
Why	—	does this visitor feel the company/department needs this solution?
What	—	solutions does the staffer feel they need?
Who	—	else is involved: final decision maker?
Who	—	else is involved: influencers?
Who	—	else is involved: financial, technical, or user buyers?
When	—	do they need information or proposal?
When	—	do they need to decide on a solution or vendors?
When	—	is the project to be completed?
When	—	must the product be delivered?
Who	—	else are they considering?
Who	—	they are doing business with now?
What	—	is their budget?
What	—	is their need in terms of units/month?
When	—	would they pay?
What	—	is their credit history?

As you can see, there is not enough time to ask this extensive list of questions, so you must limit it. Is there any way to "turbocharge" the few questions you do ask so that you get more information back than you ordinarily would? One of the ways to do this is to put "Tell me about . . ." in front of your most important qualifying questions. It makes the door to the answers open wider, letting more information flow your way.

Another turbocharged question is, "Tell me about your business." When appropriate, this question more than others brings forth a torrent of information.

Presenting the needs fulfillment solution

Now that you have taken a positive role in welcoming the visitor to your exhibit and gotten to know who you are talking to, and uncovered his or her need, it is time to show how you, your products and services, and your company can fill that need. It's time to demonstrate the product.

The most important thing you can do is prepare for presenting your needs fulfillment by anticipating the type of needs visitors will bring to you. If you are doing applications sales you especially need to carefully examine and anticipate typical user problems and how you will respond to show how your product fits. It really pays to actually rehearse these demos.

Physical demonstrations with equipment are best when kept short. A

Fig. 10-8. Two visitors listen intently as this staffer provides a benefits-oriented demonstration. He stops often to solicit feedback.

good rule of thumb for them is about three to five minutes, never going more than two minutes without asking the visitor if he or she is still with you. (See Fig. 10-8.) Remember to keep getting feedback. Many staffers think, "Now it's my turn to talk," and start talking nonstop. In fact, this step must be a dialogue between the staffer and the visitor. Staffers must stop periodically and solicit feedback from the visitor. Ask, "Does this still sound right for you?" or "Are you still with me?"

The following are six tips that can make your needs fulfillment presentations the best in the exhibit hall. Again, they seem to be simple common sense, but each is an important aspect of exhibit selling.

1. *Focus on the main need.* Don't waste your precious time on small issues; go for the main need or "hot button" instead. You find the hot button when you do a thorough job of qualifying.

2. *Be brief.* Get to the benefits and solutions fast. Don't waste time on extraneous information. Practice your presentation and keep it well under five minutes. Three is really better because then you will have more time to solicit the visitors reactions.

3. *Be solutions/benefits focused.* Forget about features. Talk problem-solving benefits.

4. *Keep getting feedback.* It can't be said often enough: get the visitor talking and let him or her talk. Ask questions and continue to probe. The more a visitor talks about his situation, the longer he will stay with you and the more you will know about him.

5. *Pause to listen.* When you ask those questions, listen hard for the answers. Shows are very noisy environments so you'll have to work hard to digest the information coming your way.

6. *Move to the close when you can.* As soon as you are getting plenty of nods of the head and other affirmations, move to closure. In an exhibit, the emphasis is not so much on selling the product as it is selling the next step in the sales cycle, which is a much easier task. Look for the very earliest opportunity to gain consensus from the visitor on taking the next step.

Closing and commitment

The final closing and commitment step has two parts to it. First, you'll need to close on the visitor's commitment to take the next step in the selling cycle. For some, that means getting a private demo, asking for a proposal, or getting references. For most exhibitors, however, it means having the visitor agree to either have a sales representative call or send literature. Again, having the visitor agree to either of those is vastly easier than trying to complete the sale right there in the exhibit.

The second part of this last step is capturing all of the qualifying information on a lead form. Most staffers wait until the very end of the conversation and then rush to write down what they remember. Instead, staffers should start writing on the lead form as early as possible. In order to do that, lead forms will need to be kept close at hand—in a pocket or on a table within arms reach.

After the lead has been written up, take the time to do two things. First, ask the visitor if there is anything else they'd like to see or if they would like a tour of the booth (if it's large enough). The second thing you need to do, and the very last interaction with the visitor, is to thank them warmly for taking time to be with you. Last impressions are important.

These are the four basic skills that you will want to work on and perfect. By doing that, you will benefit through increased numbers of leads.

Taking the time to refine these skills will pay off in the form of increased leads and sales. Practice and personalize. Think through how your own selling style, your products, or market will change these skills. Remember, you can sell rings around the competition by practicing and perfecting your exhibit selling skills—and that doesn't cost a thing but time.

Appendix A

Getting started

NOW THAT YOU'VE READ THE BOOK, HOW DO YOU GET STARTED? THIS APPEN-dix contains an easy-to-use plan that can immediately improve the results you get; things that can make a big difference immediately, beginning with the following six steps.

1. Educate your exhibit staffers.
2. Attend the right shows.
3. Use a great lead form.
4. Promote
5. Use exhibits that communicate.
6. Evaluate and fine-tune.

Educate your exhibit staffers

Having staffers who know what they're doing means you will increase the number of leads or sales you get from each show without spending a dime. But how do you get them up and running? First, have each read the chapter on exhibit selling.

Next, have them rehearse and fine-tune their selling skills, especially the welcoming skill, by role playing. It helps to have a third person observe and critique. Role playing and the critique is the single biggest factor in making staffers more productive—try it. Also, have staffers practice how they will stand.

Attend the right shows

Are you confident that you are attending the very best shows for achieving your objectives? Some exhibitors suspect that they could be missing show opportunities by not going to as many shows as they should. Others feel that they are wasting money by staying in shows at which they have exhibited for years where the results are lackluster but fear dropping out because of the impact.

First, get one of the big show directories such as Trade Show Week Data Book and analyze it for other shows you might go to. When you find one, send for the prospectus and analyze it for your target audience, as outlined in chapter 2. Be relentless in getting audits or surveys from show management and ruthless in comparing them. Then be equally ruthless in comparing those to the shows at which you now exhibit.

Typically, exhibitors spend less exhibiting at smaller shows because booth space often costs less than at big shows, and they are held in less expensive facilities, which keeps costs down. At smaller shows, you have an easier job of successfully competing for the attention of the attendees. If you can find small, geographically targeted or niche-market targeted shows, you'll be able to make a greater impact on your market and get a better return and results at lower costs. Remember, don't ever be afraid of dropping out of a show you've been in for years just because you fear that people will talk about you.

Use a great lead form

Take about a half hour and draw up a new lead form. You will benefit in three ways. First, it will act as a prompt to guide staffers when they qualify visitors. If you have worked through the qualifying question exercise in chapter 10, which prioritizes your questions, you can put them on the lead form in that order, further ensuring that the important questions are asked first.

Second, by including a rating system (A= hot lead, etc.) you will be able to very easily sort leads and prioritize them for follow-up, making sure those visitors with the most urgent needs are taken care of first.

Third, by having a place on the lead form for each bit of data, you are increasing the quality and quantity of information captured. If better information is captured, your salespeople will have better information to work with when they follow-up. That in turn will boost the quality of the follow-up process which will make you stand out from the competition.

Promote

Most shows do some promoting to get attendees to their exhibit. You can only do so much in this area, however, and are not necessarily reaching your target audience. If you want to see a specific audience, promote to them yourself.

The most straight forward and economical way to boost results through promotions is to target 50, 100, or even 150 key decision makers, who, if they came to your exhibit, would represent enough business to make the show pay off in a big way. Prior to the show, offer a premium of high perceived value, such as the brass business card case mentioned in chapter 9 in a preshow mailer. Remember, to keep the premium stored out of sight in the exhibit so as not to create hard feelings with those attendees who weren't on the list.

Most critical, have your staffers be ready to offer those hot prospects a booth tour during which they qualify and uncover their needs. These visitors are the biggest fish in your sea and worth the effort; go after them.

Use exhibits that communicate

Be absolutely 100 percent positive that your exhibit transmits the Big Three:

1. Who you are
2. What you do
3. How you can help the attendee

Keep evaluating the design and graphics messages, fine-tune and improving it. Only after this is done should you turn your attention to attractive colors and other design elements.

Evaluate and fine-tune

The "show" isn't over until you've evaluated, made some decisions about what to "tweek" and make better, and what to leave alone because it's working. Evaluate by counting leads or totalling sales and figuring cost per sale. Use this as a benchmark to compare show results. Then, when you try new promotions, you'll know if the investment has been worth it. This alone will ensure that you're light-years ahead of most exhibitors.

Follow these six steps and your trade show program will be off to a solid start. If you keep revising and fine-tuning, going over each of the steps again and again, your efforts will have a handsome pay off in increased leads or sales and a vastly greater return on your trade show investments. Try the cost saving hints in Appendix B as well, and you'll have an effective program at a very reasonable cost.

Into the realm of excellence

If you dream of a grandstand exhibiting plan that sweeps the show again and again and that puts your organization on the map and keeps it there, read on.

You have probably noticed that certain companies always make a splash, are always talked about and remembered. But how do they do it year after year? At a roundtable discussion during the exhibit industry's largest conference, five top exhibits managers sat musing about which elements in their trade show program were the ones that made the critical difference. They came up with three:

1. A lead tracking system
2. Research
3. Exhibit staff training.

In the next pages, you'll find out more about how the largest and most successful exhibitors use these particular elements to push their exhibit programs over the top and into the realm of excellence and what keeps them in the ranks of the top 10 most-remembered exhibits year after year. Your company might not have a budget the size of these top exhibitors, but you too can use each of these techniques to enhance your own image in the marketplace and make valuable contacts that result in sales.

Another look at lead tracking

Most large exhibitors have an automated lead tracking system running on one of their own computers, and all of the lead processing is done in-house. You probably won't want to devote that much time, energy, and resources to one task if you're a small exhibit or division. Besides, lead processing is usually seasonal, and in the off months when you aren't exhibiting at any shows, all of those resources are wasted. On the other hand, during the months when there are plenty of shows, everyone will go crazy trying to keep up with the work load. For those large companies going to literally hundreds of shows, an in-house lead processing resource can be kept busy all of the time. But you're not big, you're small.

A grave danger for the small company is intending to process the leads in house and then giving them the lowest priority—as fill-in work. Too often, these leads just sit in a secretary's desk drawer for weeks or even months, waiting for slack time. All the while, the leads are getting colder and colder. Having your salespeople work cold leads puts you at a competitive disadvantage, because larger companies are turning over their leads to a staff that is completely devoted to getting salespeople out in the field and the literature in the hands of the prospects.

With some planning, you too can be sure that your sales people are working the freshest, hottest leads right away—and you won't have to invest in your own in-house, dedicated lead-processing group. The following check points will assure that your lead processing system is just as sound as top exhibitors.

Who is responsible for collecting the leads and how will they get back from the show?   As you found out in chapter 6, you can never assume that the mysterious "someone" will take care of getting the leads back from the show. Remember my friend who found that 30 percent of the information stands his company rented came back with the leads still in them. If you want your leads, you must assign one reliable individual to collect them. When they do collect them, they must keep a copy to transport by hand, in case the copies that are sent get lost.

Prioritize for follow up.   This same person should also do a preliminary sorting of the leads and identify any "hot" leads which need immediate follow up within the first week after the show. If the salesperson assigned to that lead is not at the show, then the lead should be phoned or faxed to the salesperson while you are still at the show. Be assured, the big exhibitors are doing this and you don't want them to beat you to the hot prospects.

Get a lead processing service that works fast and to your specifications.   We touched on the selection of a lead processing house in chapter 6. If you are foggy on how to go about this task, now is a good time to go back and review that information. In pushing your program into the realm of excellence in this area, be sure that any lead service you choose is very responsive and will get the leads through their system and out to your salespeople within the week after the show.

This is an important point because, once those leads sit around for two weeks or more, they go stale fast. The visitors to your exhibit who requested a follow-up are now back at their office and thinking about something else or they are back there facing the exact same problem that they talked to you about at the show. In both cases, it's time to call.

I remember the first time I picked a lead fulfillment house. When I went for a site visit, the place was a mess. Boxes stacked high, leads scattered here and there. The account rep said that timing for the visit was unfortunate because they were moving to new quarters in two weeks. Impatient, I signed the contract only to find out that they were just as sloppy in their new quarters and that their work was sloppy as well. Moral of the story: if they look sloppy, they will be sloppy with your leads.

Use telemarketing to find the best prospects.   Many of the most successful exhibitors use telemarketing at some point in their lead processing. All are using the phone to get to the hot leads fast, but most also telemarket all leads to double check the qualifying data which is then used to set a priority for follow-up. These exhibitors find that when they do phone follow-up after the show, the prospect's perception of their need often changes. People who said that they just wanted a literature package will often now find that they want a salesperson to call.

One way to open this type of conversation is to say, "We are getting ready to send the literature you have requested at the show. Is there anyone else who should get literature?" That states your premise for the call, and when that question is answered, your telemarketer can go on to verify the rest of the data.

Using telemarketing for follow-up will ensure that you are putting the very best leads into the hands of your sales force as quickly as possible and in a time frame that positions you competitively with those big exhibitors. Taking the time to telemarket is especially important if your sales force is small in relationship to the number of leads or if you are using distributors and your leads compete with other manufacturer's leads. If you can show them that your leads are best, the distributors will work them first.

Pore over the reports.   Think of your lead forms as a market research questionnaire. Just by analyzing the data from the standard qualifying questions, you will have a wealth of information. You will be able to get a complete profile of who your exhibit is attracting, what they want to see, and how they intend to use your products and services.

If you have been clever in setting up your lead system and allowed for capturing of conversion-to-sale data and cross tabulation, you will be able to determine where the best and largest portion of the business is coming from, and which shows can deliver that audience to you. You can then pick the most profitable shows, drop the ones that don't pay off, and design the booth to feature just the products in which that audience is interested. This saves countless dollars wasted at the wrong shows with the wrong message and products that no one wants to see. If you do this consistently, you can clearly see trends and shifts in the marketplace—and that keeps you more competitive.

Using research

The most successful exhibitors use research in three ways. First, they are all familiar with research from the Trade Show Bureau (Denver, CO.) The Trade Show Bureau exists purely to tell us what shows can do and what to expect from them. They know what they know because they buy research from recognized research organizations specializing in the trade show area. Their research often measures the performance of shows, exhibits, or the personnel.

The second type of research used by top exhibitors measures the impact of their booth and staffers and is called a performance report. The third type of research that interests the most successful exhibitors is show performance data. Let's take a look at all three to see how you could benefit.

The Trade Show Bureau has much to offer, and you can learn much from their reports. For example, just knowing the capabilities and limitations

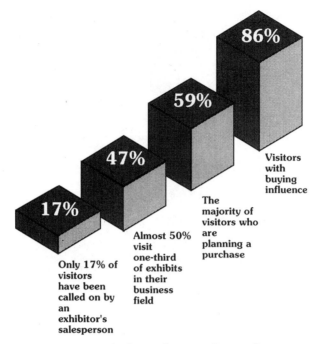

Fig. A-1. Trade shows draw quality audiences.

of this marketing communications medium is an important prerequisite to its best use. The Bureau puts out a terrific little booklet that gives just such an overview entitled, *Ten Years of TSB Reports in Ten Minutes.* The following data, and more, can be found in it.

As you can see from Fig. A-1, attendees are buyers. Eighty-six percent are visitors who are buying influencers. Curiously, only 18 percent of the average show audience has been called on in the year prior to the show.

Other research indicates that about a third of the attendees are not regular show-goers and that this is their first show. About 20 percent more missed last year's show but went the year before. Top performing exhibitors know this and look at each show as another opportunity to meet a fresh audience, a real prospecting event. You will never hear these exhibitors say, "We know everyone in our market and we just go to see our customers."

Fig. A-2 explains the number of hours that attendees spend on the show floor. Over two days, they will be on the floor more that eight hours. That averages out to about 21 minutes spent with each of the 17 exhibitors. Consequently, one of the strategies used by top exhibitors is to have in-booth activities that eat up a lot of the attendee's time, based on the theory that the more time each attendee spends with them, the less time they will have to spend with other exhibitors.

Attendees go to shows with something in mind: they want to see what's

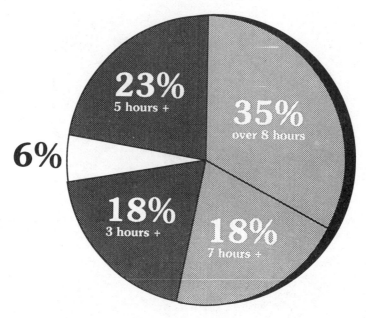

Fig. A-2. Trade show visitors spend quality time on the exhibit floor.

new. Figure A-3 illustrates that half of the typical show audience is attracted to shows because they want to see what's new. That's why you want to feature your newest products and services.

Another strategy that is a favorite with top exhibitors is to completely change the look of the booth each year, if not each show throughout the year. Because many of them use modular exhibit structures, it is easy to have a different booth layout for every show.

Additionally, most exhibitors use very high visibility promotions or themes to bring each show participation's uniqueness to life. For example, at one show, they might use a running theme and dress all of the staffers in running suits, and the next time, they change the configuration of the exhibit, the color of the carpet, and the theme and the staffers are dressed in formal wear, like tuxedos.

Those who attend shows are power people. In Fig. A-4 you can see that 29 percent of attendees are top management, and top management is an important audience. It is interesting to analyze this chart from the standpoint of tailoring your messages and graphics to the needs and wants of each of these groups. For example, top management people are interested in the economic impact that a new acquisition will have on their business, while technical buyers, like engineers, are interested in how the features and the technology of your products and services will fit into what they are already doing or planning to do. Shifting the message to suit the audience is a technique often used by top exhibitors.

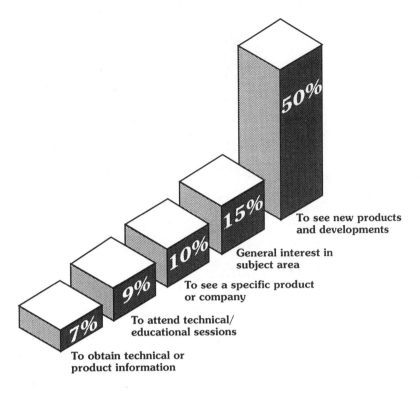

Fig. A-3. What attracts people to a trade show.

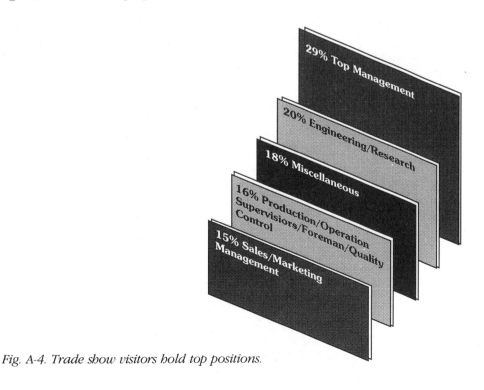

Fig. A-4. Trade show visitors hold top positions.

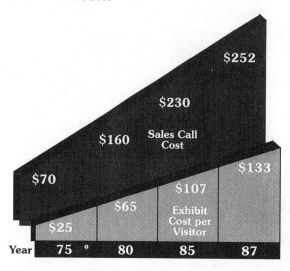

Fig. A-5. Trade shows reach prospects for less than sales calls.

Figure A-5 is especially interesting in that it compares the average cost of making an industrial sales call with the cost of seeing a visitor in an exhibit. While the costs of both have been rising, it costs almost twice as much to make a sales call as it does to see that same person at the show.

This is especially interesting when combined with the information shown in Fig. A-6 which compares the number of follow-up calls needed to close a sale. Leads taken at shows close faster because much of the selling can take place in the exhibit. Leads from other sources take longer to close, and at $252 per sales call, the difference is worth noting.

Recessions

In theory, a company should be able to reduce its cost of sale by as much as 75 percent by using only leads coming from shows. This is important news during any recession when there is a great temptation to cut back on shows in order to save money. Traditionally, the top performers deal with tough times not by cutting the show budget, but by spending the same amount at fewer shows. They use their show performance research to identify the best shows for them and then spend more at each of them.

Meanwhile, the little exhibitors are thinking about dropping out altogether or cutting way back on their show budget. Then, when the recession is over, the top performers, who have been turning up the heat by spending more at fewer shows, are well positioned to capture even larger shares of the market. Remember this when you thin, about cutting back during a recession.

Another way to use research is to hire a researcher to do a performance report that will help you evaluate the ability of your staff and your exhibit to

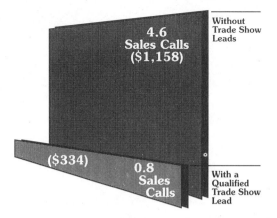

*Fig. A-6. Trade show leads
reduce sales calls and
closing costs.*

attract your target audience and satisfy their curiosity. Exhibit performance
reports are typically done by mail six weeks or more after the show, and
question attendees and visitors to your booth about their impressions about
their visit to you and your competitor's booth. They will rate your display,
products, staffers, or anything else about which you want their opinion.

Benchmarks

Top performing exhibitors use these reports to benchmark their ability to
attract the target audience (as opposed to attendees who are not the targets,)
their ability to have conversations with those targets once in the exhibit, and
the reaction of these visitors to the staffers.

   The first issue here is whether the exhibit is able to attract the right
audience. Just bring in a Paul Newman and everyone in the hall will flock to
your booth, prospects or not. That's easy. What is harder is to selectively
attract just the portion of the total attendees who are prospects for your
products and services and no one else. Top exhibitors understand this difference. What they also understand is the need for staffers to take the responsibility for starting conversations with these targets. It is useless to attract the
right people if you don't do anything with them once you bring them to your
doorstep. Therefore, one of the key pieces of valuable data from a performance report is the relationship between the percent of the target attracted
to the booth and the percent reached by your staffers.

   If the exhibit is attracting, for example, 130 percent of the audience, it is
over attracting, which means that at least 30 percent of the people in it are
not your targets. "Reach" is also important, because you could be attracting
the right people in the right amounts, but your staffers don't talk to them. In
theory, your reach and attraction rates should both be 100 percent.

   A performance report will also tell you what type of job the staffers are
doing once they reach the audience. Typically, the survey respondents will

rate them "good," "fair," or "poor." A rating of 10 percent, "poor," is considered something worth worrying about. When getting such a rating, top performing exhibitors often contract for a follow-up survey to determine the specific nature of the poor ratings. A common visitor complaint is that the staffers were not "helpful." "Helpful" can have a variety of interpretations. Usually, after thousands of dollars of additional research, they find that the problem is that staffers just haven't taken the time to adapt their usual product demos or presentations for trade shows. Show visitors are adamant about expecting that staffers know their stuff, including prices or price ranges, and can serve it up fast. They have a very low tolerance for long-winded staffers or new employees sent to the shows as a learning experience.

The type of research mentioned here, the basic exhibit performance report, costs between $1500 if shared with a number of other exhibitors and $4000 and up. It is a worthwhile investment, even if you can only do it at one show per year.

Show survey

The last category of research used by top performers is the show survey. The standard audit will give you a profile of the attendee, identifying them by title, business or industry, and geographic distribution. The survey also gives you a breakdown by product interest. It is important to note the difference: an audit gives you a profile, and a survey gives you product interest data. Although it is important to know both, it is very important to know the percent of the audience that are interested in your products and services.

Top performing exhibitors will go to great lengths to get product interest data. They will even pressure show management into paying for a survey. The route they often take is to get onto, or start, an exhibitor's advisory board. By starting one where none exists, the advisory board can present a united front that is effective in getting concessions from show management, like both an audit and a survey. If show management has an advisory board in place, the members have probably taken their seats at the invitation of show management and because of this, the board can be less aggressive in their requests.

If top exhibitors can't get show management to pay for a survey, they will ask other exhibitors to share the cost, even competitors. In this way, they are able to get and use first-class research at bargain prices.

Train the troops

Top performing exhibitors train their exhibit staffers. They can see from the research the importance of the impression made by the staffers on the target audience. Remember that 80 percent of the way the visitor feels about having been to the exhibit is based on what the staffer did while they were there. Because exhibit staff training is my business and most of these top performing companies are our clients, I can tell you exactly what they are doing with their staffers to enhance success. Here are tips taken from the top performers.

Always have a preshow meeting

Even for the smallest show, top exhibitors always have a pershow meeting at which they go over the reason they are at this particular show, their objectives for it, the exhibit and its features, the competition, latest pricing, etc. Part of the meeting reviews show selling skills, nonverbal communications and basic trade show etiquette.

Pick staffers carefully

Where these big guys slaughter everyone else is at the large shows, when they can bring in plenty of personnel. They have many employees from which to choose and can hand-pick the team they need. A surprising number have, or are, trying to go to a SWAT team approach. In this context, a SWAT team is a staffing crew that is carefully selected and used primarily at major shows. These people are put through extensive skills training and get product and industry briefings from company experts just prior to every major show. You too can approximate this approach by carefully picking staffers. When screening personnel to work the booth, be aware of these criteria:

1. Product knowledge. Are they up to speed on the very latest developments, are able to handle technical, detailed, or pricing questions? Have they thought about the problems that visitors will want to have solved and how they will respond to each? Have they run through their demonstrations or presentations, making sure they are tight and streamlined? This is no place for new hires.

2. People people. Are they extroverts? Do they enjoy talking to, and being with, people? Do they meet and work with your customers on a regular basis?

3. Industry knowledge. Are they familiar with the industry of the attendees? Do they know about major problems, regulations, issues? Can they speak the jargon, do they understand the buzzwords? Will they comprehend the visitor's problems and point of view?

4. Attitude about shows. What is their attitude about shows? Do they understand why shows are important and the role that they play in the company's marketing strategy and sales tactics? Are they aware of the objectives?

5. Previous show participation. Have they worked shows before? Do they know what's expected? What they should wear and do?

All of these criteria are important, but the first two are the most important. Staffer's shortcomings in other areas can be enhanced by training and giving them information in bulletins and memos. However, if a staffer lacks basic product knowledge and solid people skills, or is a loner, the situation is, frankly, hopeless. You can be just as aggressively competitive as the top performers by carefully selecting staffers.

Pay special attention to product demos or solutions presentations

One of the biggest secrets behind the success of top exhibitors is the care that they take with product demos and presentations. We have seen results dramatically increase and research take an upward move when staffers have the opportunity to strategize their demos and practice presentations. If you remember that the main gripe visitors have about staffers is that they lack product knowledge, then this all makes sense. But how can you benefit from this information? Do what top performing exhibitors do.

First, if you have demo stations or presentation areas, assign specific staffers to work them. Next, let them know well ahead of time that they will be working these areas and are responsible for coming up with various demos or solutions presentations in advance of the show. They should be working with a high level marketing or sales manager to identify key applications or problems that your target audience will face.

If you have more that one audience, like the economic and user buyers mentioned previously, then there will be even more preparation needed, as each will have their own set of problems. One exhibitor displayed five major products which sold to four segments of the audience, each with three to five major problems, and that meant that their staffers needed to prepare over 100 short demos. This might sound like an overwhelming number, but the demos can be brainstormed quickly if the right people get together.

Staffers must feel responsible for the visitor

The single biggest factor in achieving a quality performance really comes down to one issue: feeling responsible for the quality of the visitor's time in the exhibit. If the staffers can grasp that concept all goes well.

Your staffing team, whether large or small, should be the friendliest and easiest to talk to people on the show floor. They should make it very easy for the visitor to stop and talk and to be there with you in your exhibit. This means being out near the main traffic flow and using prepared welcoming statements to ease the visitor's entry into your exhibit and into a conversation.

Evaluate your staffers

The performance of staffers can and should be evaluated on the show floor and immediate feedback given. Some of the most dramatic improvements we've seen come when this simple technique is put to use. Simply have one or two management people evaluate all of the staffers, one at a time, rendering immediate feedback. The following criteria can be put on slips of paper, which can be used as a report card.

1. Punctuality: Arrive on time? Stay for entire shift? Return from breaks promptly?

2. Welcoming skills: Constantly busy with visitors? No more than a minute or two between visitors?

3. Nonverbals: Open stance? Good proximity to high-traffic areas? Appropriate arm and hand gestures?

4. Qualifying skills: Asks and records all qualifying questions? Before beginning the presentation?

5. Presenting skills: Keeps visitor involved by asking questions? Has planned and outlined sample demos and has anticipated the needs of most visitors? Listens vigorously to all visitor comments?

6. Closing/capturing skills: Moves quickly to commitment for follow-up? Thanks visitor? Assures visitor that a follow-up action will be taken? Fills out lead form fully and completely?

If you plan to do some coaching of staffers during the show, be sure to take a light touch. You need them to keep a positive mental outlook if you want them to do their best. They should be able to devote all of their energies to working the show and not have to worry about someone harshly critiquing them. If it is not your personal temperament to be able to offer supportive feedback, get someone else for the job.

We have had considerable success with a rally meeting on the morning of the second day. The purpose of a rally meeting is to offer additional pointers that can boost results even further—feedback—and give lots of pats on the back. Those pats are designed to be motivational and keep their energy level high and the leads coming in.

Get ready for international visitors

A surprising number of the major shows in the United States get more than 10 percent of their audience from other countries and that appears to be increasing. Dealing with a foreign audience can be a problem, however, especially if you have not given much thought to cross-cultural communications for trade shows. Increasingly, top exhibitors are seeking this information to better compete in a global market. Here is what they are finding.

Make no assumptions about anyone.   One staffer nervously approached an oriental visitor only to find that he was a Californian of Korean ancestry. The first lesson learned about communicating across cultures is that you need to suspend all values and opinions. When we rely heavily on our culturally based value systems for information, we are being ethnocentric. Being ethnocentric is the very last thing you want to be when communicating with visitors to your exhibit. Suspending judgment initially and then making judgments slowly will help your ability to evaluate each piece of information that comes your way.

Be more formal than you ordinarily might be.   Here in North America, we tend to be very casual about the use of names and titles. People from some cultures take offense at that formality, preferring instead to be called by a surname and offering their title during an introduction. In bureaucratic societies, higher-ups expect to meet with their equals, and take offense if they cannot.

Greet all visitors with the same warm smile and a, "Hello." Their response will help you determine their command of English. If you try without success to cross the language barrier, don't give up. Instead, use pantomime, point, or draw pictures. Your effort will be greatly appreciated.

For those visitors who have a light understanding of English, use the 3,000 most common words, talk slowly, and pronounciate carefully. Remember, it is often difficult for a Brooklynite to communicate smoothly with someone from the deep South, so if you have an accent, go very slowly with international visitors. Streamline language to eliminate jargon, slang, picture words, like "blue-sky thinking." Also, avoid sports terms, like "ballpark price."

If you anticipate receiving many visitors from a particular country, then it is wise to hire an interpreter. Working with one is relatively easy if you take a moment to prepare. First, brief the interpreter on your industry, products, and common industry terms. If you can, use the same interpreters repeatedly. Speak slowly and clearly, using the simple language tips mentioned previously. Feel free to state and restate. Phrasing the thought two or three ways gives it a better chance of getting across. Talk for a minute and then pause for the interpreter, letting them catch up. Use gestures just as you usually would, and by all means, keep eye contact with the subject, not the interpreter. Last, don't get concerned if they use a dictionary or make mistakes. Communicating cross culturally is an exciting challenge that should not intimidate you. Take it slowly and be patient.

Appendix B

Cost-cutting tips

THIS APPENDIX CONTAINS 77 WAYS TO TRIM YOUR EXHIBITING EXPENSES. Cost cutting is easy, really, once you know where to look.

Exhibit construction

1. Shop carefully for an exhibit builder, and when you check references, ask about costs. Do they give detailed estimates? Do they stick to those estimates?

2. Do it right the first time. If you focus on the planning stage, you'll get the exhibit you want and won't needlessly spend money because you have to fine-tune later.

3. Avoid refurbishments as much as possible. Refurbs are proportionally more expensive than the original project and should be minimized. Anticipate all of your needs and include them in the original project.

4. Protect your exhibit with good crates. By investing in well-made crates, you'll prolong the life of the exhibit. To save money, consider having them built separately according to specs by a local carpentry shop.

5. Ask your installation and dismantling firm about making any repairs to your exhibit. Some of them have a shop and can do repairs very economically.

6. Shop around for warehousing. Some installation and dismantle firms also warehouse exhibits. Compare their pricing with your exhibit house's estimate. Ask specifically what the estimate includes.

7. Consider warehousing the exhibit in your plant. If you do, be sure to anticipate how you'll handle repairs.

8. When getting estimates on exhibit construction, be certain they are complete and detailed. Estimates for exhibits should be broken down as to time and materials. Estimates for warehousing should indicate charges for moving the exhibit in and out of storage.

9. Consider buying the design separately from the construction, so that you can control the cost of both.

10. Don't do anything on a rush basis. If you wait until the last minute, it will cost 50 to 100 percent more than it would on a regular schedule.

11. Ask your exhibit builder about a discount for slow times. If you have plenty of lead time, many builders will agree to do the work during their slow seasons.

12. Consult with your exhibit builder about how to further streamline your setup. There are two times to do this: during the design stage and after the first time the exhibit is used.

13. Be sure your exhibit designer knows that cost saving is a high priority for you. Don't assume that he or she would automatically know that's your priority and keep it in mind. Some exhibitors have other priorities.

14. After your first set up of the new exhibit ask the labors to evaluate how the setup went. Inquire about any suggestions they might have about streamlining it.

15. Check the electrical wiring plans during the design phase for streamlining. If the electrician only has to make one connection, it will take less time and cost you less. Identify your electrical equipment such as junction boxes by painting your company name on them and permanently affixing them to the exhibit. This will prevent loss as well as eliminate the need to rent them.

16. Plan for a secure (locked) storage area in the exhibit. During the day, it can house purses and brief cases, and at night, it can prevent the theft of any valuables left in the booth overnight. Never put a purse under a draped table at the rear of the booth because its too easy for someone behind the booth to snatch it.

17. Consider renting an exhibit instead of buying it. Depending on your frequency of use and the cost of warehousing, it could be less expensive to rent than to buy.

18. When purchasing a modular exhibit, get a tight estimate on setup time and costs. Many can be very time-consuming to setup.

19. Keep it simple; don't reinvent the wheel. Ask your exhibit house about ready-made solutions. An example of this is a literature rack. It will cost you much more to have an exhibit house build one than it would to purchase one from a company that manufacturers retail display equipment.

20. Keep it simple and use fewer parts. Look hard at the plan for your exhibit, remembering that everything requiring assembly at the show will cost you money. Ask the exhibit house how to streamline assembly.

Planning and scheduling

21. Check the floor plan carefully, thinking about how your setup will be affected by the physical attributes of the facility. Example: must freight come up through a freight elevator, and if so, is it large enough for your exhibitry? A delay will cost you money.

22. Check the regulations concerning exhibit size to be certain that your exhibit will not pose a problem. If you have to adjust on the show floor, it will add extra hours and cost to set up.

23. If you plan to apply to show management for a variance from the regulations on exhibit dimensions, do so in plenty of time. If you automatically assume there will be no problem and go to the show without a variance, you could be made to adjust your exhibit on the show floor, and that will entail additional labor costs.

24. Some shows require that exhibitors send a sketch of the exhibit for approval. If one is requested, do send it early. If you don't, you might have to pay to adjust the exhibit on the show floor.

25. If you don't have the time to do an adequate job of planning, consider hiring a consultant to handle the logistics for you. The mistakes you make by rushing through the exhibitor's kit could easily offset the cost of a consultant.

26. Insure your exhibit. The insurance carried by your exhibit house and transportation provider don't come close to covering the total value of your exhibit.

27. Eliminate airfreight. Most exhibitors get lax with planning and ship at least some items airfreight. If you use airfreight for last minute shipments, plan better to eliminate those costs.

28. If you plan on sending literature to prospects after the show, you might not need to also send large quantities to the show. By eliminating the cost of sending it to the show, you'll save money.

29. Remove old labels. Don't risk the hazard of having your exhibit shipped to the wrong place because old labels were left on the cases. Removing the old labels eliminates the expense and inconvenience caused by delayed shipments.

30. Make transportation choices wisely. Take what you can with you and hand carry it into the hall. Materials that must be shipped should go the most cost-effective route. Be knowledgeable about transportation alternatives, then get bids on your annual schedule. Use the expertise of your corporate trafficking department if you have one.

31. Map out where your exhibitry is going to be used and then consider storing it locally instead of shipping it all the way back to the warehouse. You could save substantially on transportation costs.

On the show floor

32. Shop carefully for an installation and dismantling firm, if you use one. A good supervisor will make set up go quickly, saving you money.

33. Be there when your freight arrives, especially if you have heavy exhibitry. You need to be in the exhibit so you can tell the draymen to set the crates on the carpet line. This way, you'll save by not paying to have the carpenters move them there.

34. Save time and money during setup by reviewing setup drawings carefully with the labor crew so the workers will understand how the entire setup should proceed.

35. Be there to supervise. Don't disappear to make phone calls, etc. If there is a problem, your crew will stop until you come back with the answer. If you must make many calls, rent a cellular phone.

36. Have a "Can do," upbeat attitude when supervising your setup. Your positive leadership will get problems solved quicker and motivate the workers—and that will save money.

37. If a worker is slow to the point where it is detrimental to the efficient work schedule of your setup, make an excuse to return him to the labor pool. Wait an hour or two and announce that perhaps you need another worker after all, then go get another from the labor pool. This way, you'll avoid confrontation, which is guaranteed to slow the work.

38. Avoid tipping. While tipping to get things done fast might be tempting, in the long run, it works against the orderliness of the exhibit hall. Then too, it's expensive and results are never guaranteed.

39. If you must tip, never do it to get crates back quickly. It is unlikely that the drayman will move all 500 crates to retrieve your two in the middle.

40. Give laborers incentives. This will keep the mood up-beat and the work moving along. Caps with your company logo, coffee mugs, etc. make great incentives for staffers. If the laborers are happy, the work moves faster and your bill is lower.

41. Always sign your crew out and in, checking their time tickets when you do. Keep careful records yourself. This way, it will be easier to check the invoice for accuracy.

42. Get your work crew early in the day so that they are freshest when you review the setup drawings. If you start with them late in the day, chances are, they'll be too tired to listen carefully. If they are more efficient, your bill will be lower.

43. Check the setup schedule and plan your own setup times carefully so that you can avoid doing work on overtime. Overtime really adds to the bill.

44. Wear inexpensive, serviceable clothes to set up. Jeans and a sweat-shirt are all that are needed.

45. If you or another knowledgeable person can't be at setup, hire a supervisor. Sending a novice to coordinate setup will guarantee that it will cost you more.

46. Ask the supervisor for tips on streamlining the setup of your exhibit. Supervisors have seen plenty of setups and know all the cost-cutting tips.

47. Plan the efficient use of labor. Use fewer workers for laying the carpet, and clean up instead of wasting money by having the others just stand around watching.

48. Get service orders in prior to the deadline. Don't order them at the show where there will be a premium on them.

49. Take your own photos and save money by not using the official photographer.

50. Bring a mini vacuum and clean the booth yourself.

51. If you always rent chairs, consider buying inexpensive directors chairs. They fold up and are easily shipped. Take the backs to a tee-shirt shop that does their own screen printing and have your logo screened onto them.

52. Shop the local garden center for plants instead of renting plants at the show.

53. If you always rent large plants, consider silk plants. They could be less expensive, provided you don't find shipping them to be a problem.

54. Use a portable exhibit for the shows where you take a 10 x 10-foot or 10 x 20-foot booth. You will save on setup cost over custom exhibit setup costs.

55. Save on drayage cost by avoiding surcharges for mixed loads (where part of the shipment is crated and part is not.)

56. Ship all packages together. Packages shipped separately will each incur a minimum drayage charge.

57. Check light bulbs. Light bulbs, or for that matter anything else purchased at the show during set-up, will cost you a fortune as compared to what the same item costs at a local hardware store.

58. Identify your crates with bright colors. This will save time whenever you need to locate them. Either paint them or add bright color tape to make identification quicker.

59. File damaged claims right away. The sooner you do it, the better chance you have of actually seeing some compensation.

60. Keep good records that are easy to check. That way, whenever there is a question about what's been ordered and paid, you will be ready with the answer.

61. If you rent imprinters for the shows you go to, consider buying one. It should start paying for itself after the fifth show.

62. Print your own lead forms. Custom lead forms are very inexpensive and often cost about the same as the generic ones you can get at the show.

Space selection

63. Consider bartering for your exhibit space. Do you have a much sought-after seminar speaker who usually commands sizeable speaking fees? A product that could be used by show management? Sometimes these can be traded for booth space.

64. If a show isn't sold out, ask for a discount on the cost of the space. Many smaller shows will do this.

65. Use someone else's exhibit. If your product is being shown in an exhibitor's booth, try to provide your people as staffers. This gives you a presence without incurring the cost associated with exhibiting.

66. Can you get co-op funds from the manufacturer of products you sell and put on display in your exhibit? It could be a way to recoup a portion of your expenses.

Staffers

67. Use locals so you won't have to pay for lodging and meals. An added advantage is that they know the local customers.

68. Use local office help as hostesses. They enjoy the time out of the office and the exposure to the market and you won't have to hire temporary workers to assist at the information stand.

69. Conduct your preshow meeting in the suite, if you use one. A suite is expensive and this is an additional use for it.

70. Conduct the preshow meeting at your local office and avoid the cost of a suite or meeting room. Perhaps they have a conference room you could use. You'll avoid expensive hotel catering charges.

71. Ask show management if they have a meeting room you could use for your preshow meeting. Usually costs are minimal.

72. Play an exhibit selling skills video during the meeting. It will only cost you $20 and gets staffers familiar with how to welcome visitors, qualify, and take leads.

73. Consider sending staffers an exhibit selling skills audio tape for drive-time listening. They only cost about $10. This way, you can avoid the expense of a preshow meeting.

Show selection

74. Keep digging for more data about the shows you select. If you can pinpoint your markets and fine-tune your show list, you can save considerably by not wasting money on the wrong shows.

75. Ask your local business school library to purchase the trade show directories you need.

76. Don't be afraid to drop a show from your schedule if it's not paying off. Just do it.

77. Don't sign up until you are certain about the value of a show. It is unfortunate when exhibitors lose deposit money because they signed up too quickly.

Appendix C

What to do when

THE INFORMATION IN THIS APPENDIX CAN GIVE YOU THE INFORMATION YOU need to troubleshoot your own exhibits program and to solve problems as they happen. Here are 50 of the most common things that go wrong and what to do about them. At the end of this appendix a quick-reference chart that can help you find the solution to whatever problem is at hand.

1. Show management won't, or can't, give you the statistics you need. If you find that show management has data and won't release it, it is a safe assumption that they are afraid that you won't like it. If show management doesn't have the statistics to give you, then be vocal about telling them that show analysis data is something you need. In either case, understand that your participation in the show is a gamble.

If you do choose to exhibit, try to do some research yourself with both the visitors to your booth and those who pass by in the aisle immediately adjacent to it. You might want to question them about product interest, geography, title, and business or industry. Make your questionnaire short and easy to fill out—with check boxes.

2. A major service, like power, is not available on the show floor. An act of God or man can cause the power to go out, or a snowstorm can close the roads and airports. While there's not much you can do to stop the snow or turn the power back on, you can ask show management for either a rebate on your booth space charge, or a discount on next year's space. They know that under the terms of the contract, you probably are not entitled to it, but are often willing to give back a little to ease your disappointment.

3. Your crates won't fit in the elevator. In this situation, which happens at hotels, the first thing to do is inquire about a freight elevator that is larger. If that doesn't work out, unload the exhibitry on the ground floor and bring the pieces up without the crates. Also, check to see if the trap door in the ceiling of the elevator can be removed, making it possible to stick the tallest panels out of the top.

4. The roof of the exhibit hall leaks. First, unplug all of the electrical equipment. Be careful but do this quickly. Next, move any exhibitry that you can by hand, then cover the biggest pieces with plastic sheets. Get the plastic used to protect carpeting during set up, or plastic garbage bags, split open and taped together. Now, get your heaviest pieces moved to a safe place.

As soon as you can, notify show management about the problem. When things settle down a bit, locate a wet vac to suck up the water from your carpet. Finally, talk to show management about them paying for any charges, like the plastic sheets and the wet vac service, as well as any damage to your exhibit.

5. The show is sold out and you can't get space. Getting a presence at the show without being on the floor can be done. Try some of these strategies. First, provide your personnel as speakers for the conference program. To do this, call the conference chairman and suggest a new topic, with your speaker. Second, get together with exhibitors on the show floor by providing equipment, signage, and personnel. Next, get a suite at a nearby hotel and offer a seminar or demo and use direct mail to publicize it. You could also host a very unusual social event. All of these will get you some visibility when you don't have a booth.

6. The computer equipment doesn't show up. Computer equipment is very easily rented nationwide. Look in the yellow pages or ask the show manager, the furniture rental service, or the audio/visual service at the show for a reference.

7. Your shipment doesn't arrive. The first thing to do is check at the drayage desk for any record of receiving it. If it arrived, then get them and yourself busy checking in the hall. If not, call your transportation provider with the bill of lading number. If your exhibit house arranged for shipping, be sure you know the bill of lading number, and have the phone number of the transportation provider. Next, have a tracer put on the shipment and be specific when you ask them to get back to you. Be sure you have the name of the person you talk to and set a time when the two of you will speak again. Meanwhile, start thinking about what you will do if your exhibitry doesn't show up.

8. Your exhibit doesn't show up. After you have gone through all of the steps outlined in Step 7, consider whether you can make a joke out of your misfortune, and do as one exhibitor did: Get a big funeral wreath with a sash reading, "In Honor of Our Exhibit: Missing In Action."

For a more serious solution, try renting an exhibit from a local source, like the furniture rental service or a local exhibit house. Check the yellow pages for listings and ask around at the show. Another solution is to fill the booth space with plants and, using rental furniture, create an inviting space for conferencing.

9. Freight unloading is always very slow. If unloading is slow at a show, there could be any number of reasons, but if it is always very slow, it might be that your driver is missing important information. Be sure that your transportation provider has, and is using, the following information: show name, exhibitor name, booth number, number of pieces, crated or uncrated, and special problems or schedules associated with unloading at the site, or when special arrangements have to be made. Also, be sure that the driver has the name of a contact at the show city, for instance you or your installation supervisor's name and local phone number so that he can contact you should something go wrong.

10. Your space has been changed. The show revised the layout of the hall, and you don't find out until you get on site. When you get to the show and you have a new booth location and weren't informed prior to the show, you have two issues to deal with. First, you need to decide if the new space assignment is acceptable to you. Take a good look around and decide if the new space is comparable to the old location. If not, talk to show management.

Next, consider that all of your freight and service orders will have the old booth number on time. Visit all of the service desks and get the booth number changed on the order forms. Then when something is missing, remember that the first place to look is the old location.

11. Your literature shipment does not arrive. Briefly look for the shipment in the usual places by checking with the drayage desk and walking the floor. Don't waste too much time before doing whatever you need to do to get more sent. If all else fails, take one piece and have a copy service run off a few copies.

12. One laborer performs poorly. When one laborer performs poorly, his or her actions can slow everyone down, so you want to get rid of him as soon as possible without a fuss. The easiest route is to simply make a big point of telling all of the workers that the crew is one person too large and that you must return someone to the labor pool. After returning the lazy worker to the pool, wait an appropriate amount of time, an hour or so, and announce that, on second thought, there is a need for another worker. Then go get one from the labor pool.

13. There is no record of the services you ordered. If you get to the show and check at the service desk to find that they have no record of your orders and prepayment, it's too late to do much. First, you should have checked two weeks prior to the show to make certain that the orders were received and there was no problem with them. You also should have a site book with you, with a copy of the forms and deposit checks. If you have no site book and no way to prove that you did place the order, then you will have to place the order at the show, pay the premium, and be put at the end of the line. Ask if, when you get back to the office and you get a copy of the previously sent service form and check, will they give you a refund of the difference between the discounted order cost and the higher one placed at the show.

14. The bolt box needed for your custom exhibit is empty. This happens all of the time when exhibitors do not stay for tear down. Once the exhibitor leaves, so do the bolts, which are then re-sold to the next group of exhibitors who are also missing their bolts. Stay for tear down, but if you are still missing bolts during setup, know that you will pay less for them and slow down the bolt theft circle by buying them out of the hall.

15. There is very little time between shows. In the case of a quick turn-around from one show to the next, communication is imperative. Make certain that your bill of lading and labels for the outbound shipment are ready, and as usual, you have removed all of the old labels. Check and double check to be sure that drayage knows your situation and can keep your crates handy and ready at close of show and that your outbound transportation provider is alerted and waiting as well.

16. There is damage done to your exhibit during set up. The first step is to identify who did the damage. There is little hope for filing a legitimate damage claim if you don't know who did the damage. If you do know who did it, then go to the appropriate service desk and file a damage report. The key to getting your claim taken care of is to get the damage fixed at the show, if possible, or to get a written estimate while you are still at the show from which they can pay immediately. Once you come back from the show, it's easy for people to forget your claim. There is less urgency since you have undoubtedly already paid their bill.

17. There is damage to the exhibit from an unknown source. In this case, unlike step 16, you have no recourse. That's why you must be sure that your exhibit is insured under your corporate policy. Never depend on the insurance of the carriers, the exhibit house, or the show manager to cover your losses. It just doesn't go far enough.

18. Missing lead cards. This one is easy. Just get three-by-five-inch cards from the stationery supply store. If they are closed, ask at the front desk of the hotel.

19. The sales reps don't follow up on leads. If you find that your sales reps don't follow up on the leads fast enough or at all, there could be a variety of reasons. First, are the leads any good? It could be that your lead card needs refinement to better capture the right information. Next, are the leads getting to them in a timely manner? No one wants to work leads from a show that happened six months ago because the leads will be cold. Check that there is a place on the lead forms to indicate time frame of purchase. This will help the sales reps prioritize their follow up. A rating system will also help prioritize leads; "A" for hot leads, "B", follow up next, and "C", indicating literature only.

If your sales reps are really overloaded or your leads are going on to distributors who will pick and choose amongst the leads from many manufacturers, think about giving them to a telemarketing firm for the first phase of follow-up. This way, only pre-screened leads will go out to the field.

20. Your custom-color carpet doesn't show up. Although you can easily rent standard carpet from the official show contractor, the color and quality are common looking and these won't give you the special look that you get with custom carpet. Instead, try to borrow carpet from your "friends." Call your exhibit house, local exhibit houses and other exhibitors and describe the type of carpet you need.

21. Can't find out about small regional or local shows. Try local chapters of the national associations, visitors and convention bureaus, and the local facilities where shows might be held.

22. Arrive at the show to find that your space is in the worst location and will not get any traffic. Get attendees to your booth with smell. Rent a popcorn maker and the smell will pull in traffic from all over the hall.

23. Something is stolen from your exhibit. Make sure that it is stolen and not just misplaced. Items of value can get put back in crates or hidden under something, especially during setup. If it was stolen, report it to the police and show management. Next time, secure valuables in locked areas and get insurance.

24. Workers hassle you about setting up your exhibit. If your exhibit can be set up in under 30 minutes without tools, then you are within your rights to set it up yourself. Feel free to complain to show management if you are hassled.

If it takes you longer than a half hour, then the workers have jurisdiction over your setup and can take over. If you run over the time limit by just a few minutes, chances are that you won't be bothered. If it takes you considerably longer than the half hour, then it is very likely that someone will point out that the union has jurisdiction over the work that you are doing. The best thing to do is not argue and go get a labor crew to finish up. If you refuse to hire union labor, are stubborn, or make a scene, it is likely that you will be made to have the laborers take down the work you have done and start over—all at union rates and very slowly.

25. Need to find a builder for a new exhibit. If you need a new exhibit, the first thing to do is set some objectives for it. There are physical criteria, like size, use of logo, storage, etc., and there are marketing criteria, like audience served, psychographics, product position, etc. which need to be identified.

Once that is done, you are ready to look for a supplier. One of the very best ways to do this is to walk the show floor to identify exhibits that you think are working well. Then, talk to their owners to find out who designed and built them. Ask would they use them again and, if so, what would they do differently.

Most exhibitors like to interview about three suppliers in the initial review stage of an exhibit design project. Later, after the interview, they will narrow it down to just one.

Other sources of exhibit designers and builders are *Exhibitor Magazine's Directory* (Exhibitor Publications, Rochester, Minnesota) and the yellow pages.

26. The drayage bill seems high. In this situation, check the invoice thoroughly against the weight ticket to be certain that you are being billed accurately. Remember, drayage is billed by the hundred weight.

27. The exhibit staffers don't show up on time or at all. There are two remedies for this problem. First, make sure that you have a booth duty schedule and that everyone has a copy. You might even want to post it in the booth, at the information stand or on the back or inside of the exhibit structure, such as in a coat closet or briefcase storage area.

Next, get a booth duty captain, preferably someone in sales management, who is responsible for the staffers. The captain should tell the staffers that, if they can not make their scheduled duty period, they are responsible for finding a replacement.

If you are using distributors to staff your exhibit, expect that their reliability will depend on your relationship with them, and if you are in control, they will show up, but that if you are not, they will not.

28. Not enough staffers. If, for whatever reason, you find that you do not have enough staffers to work the exhibit, think about augmenting the work load with some rented help. While temporary personnel will not be able to answer complex product questions, they can function effectively as greeters who screen visitors and handle them until an employee staffer is available.

29. Staffers don't talk to visitors. The first question to ask is, do they know what to do? If not, have them read the chapter on exhibit selling and discuss it. Next, have them role play welcoming people into the exhibit.

30. Staffers spend too much time talking to each other. Again, as with the problem in step 29, the staffers may not know what else is required of them so they do what feels comfortable, which is chatting with each other. As a remedy, be sure that they know the exhibit selling skills and how to use them. If they do and still persist in chatting too much, then get a booth captain to keep an eye on them.

Another possibility, especially for a far-flung field sales force, is that they might actually need time to network with each other. In this case, try a dinner the night before the show opens.

31. The design of the exhibit has no "punch." Look at your exhibit and check that it is communicating the Big Three: who you are, what you do, and how you can help the visitor. If not, start there. Beyond these, think about using color, motion, or sound to attract attention. Building one of these into the design scheme will increase the impact of your exhibit. Just be sure it ties in with your theme or product.

32. The price quote on the new exhibit is too high. If you have already checked the quote to be sure there is no simple mistake, then consider whether you can go without crates. If you are already shipping part of the exhibit loose or some equipment without crates, then you will pay no more to send the exhibit pad wrapped. If you are thinking about going without crates, be sure to add the drayage surcharge into your comparison.

Another alternative is to build what you can afford now and postpone some of those expensive details, like product pedestals or literature stands, until later.

Ask about having the exhibit built during slow times. Most exhibit houses have seasonally slow periods and, if given enough lead time, will consider building an exhibit when the shop is not very busy. If you are going to go this route, you need to plan well in advance.

Last, think about using a modular or portable display instead of a custom exhibit. It could cost less.

33. The design presented by the exhibit house is not satisfactory. In this situation, and assuming that you conveyed your objectives to the designer, ask for a meeting with the designer and the account executive. In the meeting, review the objectives and point out where the design they have submitted could better meet each of your objectives.

Keep your comments phrased positively, not negatively. Avoid negative statements like, "These graphics are dull." Instead, use positive language like, "Our product is very exciting and I'd like to see that excitement in the graphics, too." Have this conversation with the designer and not just the account executive. When you are not getting the design you want, it is very important to communicate directly with the designer.

34. The show leads come back to the office and sit there for a few weeks. It is important to follow up on leads as soon as possible. Remember, you are competing with other exhibitors for the attention of those special visitors, and that extends past the show into follow-up time.

Get your follow-up plant in place well before the show. Ask who is responsible for collecting and transporting the leads, sorting them, and getting them out to the field sales force? What literature will be sent? All of these questions should be answered before you leave for the show. By having a system in place, you are ensuring that leads won't just sit around.

35. The exhibit space is undesirable. If you find that the space you have been assigned is undesirable and puts you at a competitive disadvantage, then voice your concerns to show management. Try to get them to see it from your point of view. Tell them why it is important for your company to have another space. Keep calling back periodically to check for vacancies caused by cancellations.

36. Dropping out of a show with no negative impact. First, be clear about your reasons for dropping out and state them in the most positive way possible. For example, if there is a budget cutback, your public statement should be that you have decided to spend the funds elsewhere. When you have carefully crafted a public statement about your reasons for dropping out, waste no time in getting that message out to your sales and marketing people—anyone who has contact with the public should know the reason for dropping out.

37. A booth obstruction not on the floor plan. First, take your floor plan, which should be in your site book, to the show manager to register a complaint and inquire about moving your booth to a better location. If none is available, then negotiate for a rebate on the space cost. At the same time, start thinking about how to either incorporate the column, fire box, or other obstruction into the layout of the exhibit or camouflage it. Two of the most common ways of hiding a column are by draping it or screening it with tall plants; then petition show management to pay the costs.

38. Staffers pay show services invoices. Typical of this problem is the instance when show services personnel arrive in your booth to demand immediate payment of an invoice. Staffers, trying to do the right thing, will often be pressured into paying without checking for accuracy, or worse, pay when the invoice has already been paid. To avoid this problem, make certain that you personally have arranged for payment of all invoices. Next, tell staffers never to sign for any payments. Instruct them to give your name as the individual in charge of payments.

39. Must pay invoice before leaving the hall. If you have read the exhibitors kit, you will be aware of payment policies, which always indicate that you must make credit arrangements. Typically, the smaller exhibitors send payments in advance or plan to pay by credit card. Whatever additional services ordered at the show must be paid for prior to the close of the show, the method of payment is company check, credit card, or travelers checks.

40. The best way to evaluate a new show. After you have considered the statistical analysis of the show, the best way to get a feeling for the show is to walk through it as an attendee. Call show management to request a pass and then walk the aisles talking to attendees and exhibitors alike.

41. Can't read the handwriting on the lead forms. This a very common problem that can be disastrous to the follow-up process. To solve it, ask staffers to print all information on the lead form and to sign it. Then use a booth captain to check all of the leads hourly. This way, he or she can catch any missing information or illegible writing as soon as it happens and before the staffer forgets.

42. The best way to handle the stress of setup. To lessen the stress associated with setup, make sure you have spent ample energy on the planning process. If you have an updated site book, followed your schedule, and sent in and checked on orders for service, then irregularities during setup will be minimized. If something goes wrong, rely on the experts, like the show manager or the service people, and don't be shy about asking other exhibitors for advice.

Prior to the show, take some time to think about what you would do if disaster struck and your exhibit, product or literature didn't show up. These are just about the worst disasters that happen to any exhibitor, and having a back up plan for each of them will make you feel less stressed.

Last, when you feel your temper getting short, get off the floor, take a nap, read a book, or go for a swim or massage. Taking a break will help you put things in perspective.

43. Can't get good (any) hotel rooms. First, ask how the hotel rooms are assigned. Some show managers give attendees preference over exhibitors and the result is that attendees end up at the better hotel and the exhibitors are at another, less desirable hotel. Other show managers try to keep an even mix of attendees and exhibitors, but give preference to larger exhibitors and put them in the better hotels. Most just assign them on a first-come-first-served basis, however.

Once you understand the system used to assign sleeping rooms at the show, try to comply. If you still don't get the hotel of your choice, it might be time to go outside the system. One tactic used by exhibitors is to have a travel agent call the hotel directly and book reservations for individuals, not using the company name or the conference discount. You will end up paying more for the rooms and won't be able to book many of them at any one hotel, but you will have a better chance of placing a few of your people in the right hotels.

44. Always late getting the service orders placed. Understand that when you send in service orders late, you end up paying a premium for them. The remedy for this problem is a schedule. Read your exhibitor kit thoroughly as soon as you get it and post all of the service order due dates on it.

45. Controlling distributors who work in your exhibit. To a large extent, your relationship with your distributors determines how they perform in the exhibit. If you are in control of the distributors and have a strong position with them, then they are likely to show up on time, stay in the booth, and get leads for you. If you have a weak relationship, they are likely to show up when they please and do as they wish when in the booth. In either case, there are things that you can do to improve their performance.

If you have a strong relationship, then set a booth duty schedule for them and have a booth captain to whom they report. Tell them that if they are to work in your exhibit, you expect their full cooperation.

If your relationship is not very strong, then move from the "stick" approach above, to this "carrot" approach. Offer them an incentive for performing within your guidelines, which includes a booth duty schedule. The carrot might be a discount on products, show specials, or the leads, as well as the traditional incentives or "spiffs," like prizes, travel, and entertainment.

46. Top management's role in the exhibit. The presence of the top guy or gal can either cause the exhibit to hum with activity or all activity to halt as he or she holds court. Top management needs to have a role and someone needs to tell him or her exactly what that role is.

If this is your problem, have a private conversation with him and explain that you noticed that all positive lead gathering activity stops when he comes into the exhibit because the staffers flock to his side. Then ask if he, too, has a problem with that. Invariably, he will and this will give you an opportunity to speak at length about a more productive role for your leader.

Typically, the role that top managers play is to stay available to meet with the press, key customers, and important prospects. Some even choose to take a short turn at booth duty so that they can remain in touch with the buying public.

47. Can't get press coverage. If you want to get press coverage, and trade shows are a great place to do that, start by assigning one person to the task. Have them compile a list of key press people who will be at the show, then call each to set up an appointment for a personal booth tour. Press kits can be left in the press room, but many exhibitors choose to have them available in the exhibit.

It is also very important to follow up with the press after the show so that you can answer any questions. By getting in touch with key individuals and staying in touch, you will be able to increase the press coverage that you receive.

48. Staffers talk to the press and say the wrong things. If this has happened to you, then you have probably reprimanded the guilty staffers to the point where everyone is afraid to say anything, even hello, to anyone with a press badge.

The real problem is to get staffers to say the right thing to the press. First, make sure that all staffers know what color badges are assigned to the press. Next, tell them to watch for the press and to greet them warmly. If you can, identify one person to be responsible for the press and act as your press relations manager at the show. Last, review the official company statements and policies on sensitive issues in your preshow meeting.

49. Having trouble understanding the exhibit house invoices. You should receive a detailed estimate at the start of every project. This estimate should be broken down by time and materials and the invoice should then reflect the estimate. Problems occur when the original estimate is not properly broken down as to time and materials, when the invoice does not reflect the estimate, or when there is no estimate. Explain to the exhibit house that you need, and must have, a completely detailed estimate and that they must alert you by phone and in writing at any time the job deviates from the estimate.

50. Need an inexpensive mailer. One of the most successful preshow promotional mailers is the post card. They have a high readership rate and are inexpensive to print and mail.

Quick Reference Chart

Show Selection

1   No statistics available.
5   Show is sold out.
21   Locating small or regional shows.
36   Dropping out of a show.
40   Evaluating new shows.

Setup

2   No power or other major services.
3   Crates don't fit in the elevator.
4   Roof leaks.
6   Missing computer equipment.
7   Shipment doesn't arrive.
8   Exhibit doesn't arrive.
9   Slow freight unloading.
11   Literature doesn't arrive.
12   Laborer performs poorly.
13   No record of show services ordered.
14   No bolts.
15   Quick turnaround between shows.
16   Damage during setup.
17   Damage by unknown source.
20   Missing carpet.
23   Something stolen.
24   Problems setting up your own booth.
37   Obstructions not on floor plan.
42   Handling stress of setup.
44   Late service orders.

Leads

18   Missing lead cards.
19   No follow-up.
34   Slow processing after the show.
41   Can't read handwritting.

Exhibit

25   Locating an exhibit builder.
31   Design lacks punch.
32   High-price quotes.
33   Unacceptable design.

Expenses

26   Checking drayage bills.
38   Staffers pay show service invoice.

Index

OTHER BESTSELLERS OF RELATED INTEREST

IMPORT/EXPORT: How to Get Started in International Trade—Carl A. Nelson

This excellent starter guide is for anyone who wants to get in on the excitement, the prestige, and the profits of doing business around the world. Nelson relates real-life success stories and proven tips, including his 20 keys to success. You'll find all you need to turn your entrepreneurial spirit into a fascinating and profitable business. 208 pages, 53 illustrations.

Book No. 30052, $14.95 paperback only

DIRECT MARKETING COUPON DESIGNS: 300 Creative Copyright-Free Camera-Ready Professional Layouts—CLIP AWAY™

A collection of ready-to-use coupons, campaign themes, and design guidelines that will help you create productive coupon programs quickly and easily. Use the samples straight from the book. Mix and match. You get type, typefitting, paper, and ink information along with an anthology of sample coupons from the marketplace. Plus you'll find tips on writing persuasive copy and graphics, and trackers to chart the success of your campaigns. 208 pages, illustrated.

Book No. 3482, $19.95 paperback only

GETTING OUT: A Step-by-Step Guide to Selling a Business or Professional Practice—Lawrence W. Tuller

A management consultant and former business owner, the author brings 25 years of buyout and acquisition experience to bear on the problems of establishing a "getting-out" position. He offers a complete and authoritative treatment of the subject for owners of any size business—as well as doctors, lawyers, accountants, and other professionals in private practice. 320 pages, 30 illustrations.

Book No. 30063, $24.95 hardcover only

RETIRE IN STYLE—The Lifetime Security Planning Guide—Edward S. Soltesz

Here is a comprehensive guide to retirement planning that can help ensure financial security for your golden years. Soltesz shows you how to build a secure retirement nest egg. Step-by-step guidance, examples, and worksheets are supplied for planning your successful retirement. Specific advice for people already retired is also presented. 300 pages.

Book No. 30017, $15.95 paperback only

THE PERSONAL TAX ADVISOR: Understanding the New Tax Law—Cliff Roberson, LLM, Ph.D.

How will the new tax law affect your tax return this filing season? Any reform is certain to mean a change in the way your taxes are prepared. But you don't have to be an accountant or a lawyer to understand the new tax laws . . . use this easy-to-read guide and learn how to reduce your income taxes under the new federal rules! 176 pages.

Book No. 30134, $12.95 paperback only

MONEY MINDER: Simplify, Organize, and Manage Your Personal Financial Records—Michal E. Feder and Martin L. Ernst

"I like [the book's] flexibility. The forms encourage you to think creatively and profitably about how you are spending and investing your money."
                                        —Jean Ross Peterson
Author of *Organize Your Personal Finances*

Offers an excellent, streamlined method for straightening out your finances. This book offers step-by-step guidance and ready-to-use forms that will enable you to consolidate important financial facts and figures in one place. 128 pages, 88 illustrations.

Book No. 30039, $12.95 paperback only

INSTANT LEGAL FORMS: Ready-to-Use Documents for Almost Any Occasion
—Ralph E. Troisi

By following the clear instructions provided in this book, you can write your own will, lend or borrow money or personal property, buy or sell a car, rent out a house or apartment, check your credit, hire contractors, and grant power of attorney—all without the expense or complication of a lawyer. Author-attorney Ralph E. Troisi supplies ready-to-use forms and step-by-step guidance in filling them out and modifying them to meet your specific needs. 224 pages, illustrated.

Book No. 30028, $16.95 paperback only

HOW TO INCORPORATE YOUR BUSINESS IN ANY STATE—Hoyt L. Barber

Now you can form your own corporation in any state without bureaucratic hassles or expensive legal fees. Everything you need—including filing forms and other legal forms for all 50 states—has been included in this hands-on guide. 144 pages, illustrated.

Book No. 30044, $9.95 paperback only